REPORT NO. 9

THE NEGRO
IN THE BANKING INDUSTRY

by

ARMAND J. THIEBLOT, JR.

Assistant Professor of Management
College of Business and Public Administration
University of Maryland

Published by

INDUSTRIAL RESEARCH UNIT, DEPARTMENT OF INDUSTRY
Wharton School of Finance and Commerce
University of Pennsylvania

Distributed by

University of Pennsylvania Press
Philadelphia, Pennsylvania 19104

Copyright © 1970 by the Trustees of the University of Pennsylvania
Library of Congress Catalog Card Number 77-103-334
Manufactured in the United States of America
SBN:8122-9048-8

FOREWORD

In September 1966, the Ford Foundation announced a major grant to the Industrial Research Unit of the Wharton School to fund studies of the Racial Policies of American Industry. The purpose of the research effort, now in its fourth year, is to determine why some industries are more hospitable to the employment of Negroes than are others and why some companies within the same industry have vastly different racial employment policies, and to propose appropriate policy.

The studies have proceeded on an industry by industry basis, under the direction of the undersigned, with Dr. Richard L. Rowan, Associate Professor of Industry, as Associate Director. This study of the banking industry is the ninth in a series of reports dealing with specific industries; others already published include the automobile, aerospace, steel, hotel, petroleum, rubber tire, chemical, paper, and meat industries. Studies of the insurance, tobacco, public utilities, motor, rail and air transport industries, among others, are scheduled for completion soon. We expect also to publish major studies combining and comparing the findings of the various industry studies.

This report on the banking industry is the work of Dr. Armand J. Thieblot, Jr., Assistant Professor of Management at the University of Maryland's College of Business and Public Administration. Dr. Thieblot presented the study as his doctoral dissertation at the University of Pennsylvania. He had previously earned a B.S. in Aeronautical Engineering from Princeton University and an M.B.A. from the Wharton School of Finance and Commerce, University of Pennsylvania. While earning his doctorate, he served as a Lecturer on the Wharton faculty and as a Research Associate in the Industrial Research Unit, distinguishing himself both as a teacher and as a researcher. His study of the *Negro in Banking* is the result of eighteen months' work, during which he visited banks in major cities throughout the country.

Many persons assisted in the making of this study. Dr. John R. Coleman, President of Haverford College, and a former member of the Ford Foundation staff, made the original grant possible. Foremost among the numerous bankers, government agency officials, and other interested persons who gave freely of their time are Mr. Robert C. Albright, of the American Bankers Association, and Mr. David A. Sawyer, of the U. S. Department of the Treasury. The manuscript was typed by Mrs. Louise Morrison. Mrs. Marjorie Denison and Miss Elsa Klemp edited the manuscript, proofread it, and constructed the index. Mrs. Margaret E. Doyle, Administrative Assistant for the Industrial Research Unit, handled the various administrative duties and details for this, as for other Industrial Research Unit projects. A special note of thanks is due the author's wife, Bernice, who assisted in numerous ways. The author, of course, accepts sole responsibility for the content.

In most previous reports, as in this one, the data cited as "in the author's possession" have been carefully authenticated and are on file in the Industrial Research Unit library.

HERBERT R. NORTHRUP, *Director*
Industrial Research Unit
Wharton School of Finance and Commerce
University of Pennsylvania

Philadelphia

March 1970

TABLE OF CONTENTS

VIII.   BANKING ACTIVITIES IN SUPPORT OF INCREASED NEGRO
            PARTICIPATION 137

         Affirmative Action 137

         Recruiting 142

         Selection.. 145
            Testing 146

         Training 149
            "Hard-Core" Programs 150
            Relationships to Schools 153

         Other Banking Activities... 154

         Summary... 155

  IX.   POLICY STATEMENTS 156

         Equal Employment Policy Statements 156

         Affirmative Action Statements... 159

   X.   DETERMINANTS OF INDUSTRIAL POLICY 162

         Initial Response.. 163
            Job Characteristics.. 163
            Image... 163

         Accelerating Acceptance on Clerical Levels 164
            Lack of Artificial Barriers 164
            Drawbacks 166

         Continued Lack of Action on Managerial Levels........... 167
            Caution 167

         Internal Divergence 168
            Communications.. 168
            Managerial Reactions... 168

         Concluding Observations 169

Appendix

LIST OF TABLES

APPENDIX TABLES

LIST OF FIGURES

CHAPTER I.

Introduction

Although the banking industry is one of the mainstays of the American economy and has always been a necessary partner in new movements in technology and industrialization, it has not been on the forefront of social change. Banking was among the last of the country's major industries to abandon traditional hiring practices and make available responsible job opportunities to Negroes. Not until 1962 or 1963 did the industry begin a noticeable program of hiring Negroes. But once begun, in at least the largest of the nation's banking establishments, the program has been pursued vigorously.

The reasons for banking's long delay are many. On the part of banks themselves, inexperience with untrained job applicants (of whom many are Negroes), fear of a loss of accounts or other reaction from either customers or employees, and a misplaced conception of the prestige image of the industry all had their effect. Many potentially qualified Negro job applicants were undoubtedly deterred by the nature and image of the industry, its level of skills demanded for even entry-level jobs, and its historical hiring patterns. There are many other factors.

The study is concerned with the evolution and present status of Negro employment policies in the banking industry. Basic to an understanding of the acceptance of Negroes by the industry is the nature and structure of the industry itself, which is discussed in the next chapter.

CHAPTER II

Structure of the American Banking Industry

The history of the American banking industry has been a history of change, for the industry has always been closely associated with the changing requirements and demands of a rapidly evolving economy. The product of the industry is credit, and the demand for credit takes many forms. From the waning years of the eighteenth century through the beginning of the twentieth century America was expanding in all directions. Merchants and traders, the westward moving farmers, the transportation system which had to be built to tie the two together, manufacturers, suppliers, and the general public all wanted credit. And banks arose to fill the need.

By 1820, only forty years after the founding of the country's first bank in Philadelphia, 300 banking institutions were in active operation Twenty years later, there were over 1,000, and by 1860, there were more than 2,000. The numerical peak of 30,900 commercial banks was reached in 1920.

For all its growth and spread in every financal direction, banking remained essentially an infant industry until the mid-1930's. "On the whole, the banking system mirrored the society as a whole—diverse, disorderly, growing rapidly but at an uneven pace of fits, jerks, and starts—enterprising and progressive, but not always overly scrupulous." [1] With relatively easy entry into the industry over most of its history, and with the lure of high profits from the endless credit needs of the burgeoning country—and lacking the machinery to avoid emphasizing swings in the business cycle—the industry contributed heavily to depressions and panics which seemed to come with distressing frequency. Severe banking panics, actually attributable to a wide variety of causes but almost always associated with a general distrust on the part of the American population of its banking system, occurred in 1837, 1857, 1873, 1884, 1893, 1903, 1907, 1919, 1929, and 1933.

---

[1] Paul B. Trescott, *Financing American Enterprise* (New York: Harper & Row, 1963), p. 38.

The failure and forced closings of banks was a serious factor in the industry from its inception until about 1935. It is estimated that one-half of all banks founded between 1810 and 1820 had failed by 1825, and one-half of those founded between 1830 and 1840 had met a similar fate by 1845. In this century between 1920 and 1929, generally considered to be years of previously unparalleled prosperity, 5,411 banks failed, an average of about 600 per year.[2] More than 5,000 failed between 1930 and 1932, and the overall attrition was such during the depression that in 1939, only 14,770 banks remained in operation of the more than double that total which had been in operation twenty years previously.[3]

The industry matured following the stabilizing effect of the Federal Deposit Insurance Corporation, founded in 1934, and since that time the number of bank failures has decreased greatly. There have been fewer than 400 since 1934, and from the end of World War II, failures have averaged only about two a year. The number of banks (including mutual savings banks) in operation as of June 29, 1968, was 14,183, and most of the more recent numerical decreases have arisen from mergers.

Regulation

Regulation of the banking industry has taken many forms through the years, and the demands for tighter or looser control have often caught up the entire country in controversy. The first real trial of the powers of the federal government over the states, which culminated in Chief Justice Marshall's famous decision in the *McCulloch* v. *Maryland* case, involved the constitutionality of a tax imposed by the State of Maryland on the Baltimore branch of the second Bank of the United States.

This was essentially an argument of whether the philosophies of Jefferson or those of Hamilton would have sway in determining the structure of the nation, but as a side effect, it also concerned whether the country would have a central bank or a

---

[2] Charles R. Whittlesey, Arthur M. Freedman, and Edward S. Herman, *Money and Banking: Analysis and Policy* (New York: The Macmillan Company, 1963), p. 532.

[3] The American Bankers Association, *The Story of American Banking*, a pamphlet prepared by the Banking Education Committee of the Association (New York: The American Bankers Association, 1963), p. 66.

diversified system of state banks. The argument was settled in 1803 in favor of national banks and a national currency. This was done without destroying the state banking system but by imposing a tax of 10 percent on all further issues of bank notes other than those authorized by the National Currency Act of 1862, and providing certain other benefits to banks willing to adopt national charters.

The National Banking Act of 1863 attempted to work through incentives rather than prohibitions, and added stability to the banking system without destroying its flexibility. Nevertheless, it had many inadequacies. It did not provide a central banking system, and continued to allow the pyramiding of deposits and other practices which proved to be incendiary in the event of economic downturns, often fanning them into full-scale panics or depressions.

Not until December 1913, when President Wilson signed the Federal Reserve Act into law, was a workable national framework constructed within which a viable commercial banking system could operate. The founding of the Federal Deposit Insurance Corporation in 1934, completed the major legislative activities.

What cannot be detailed here is the complexity and the fantastic profusion of permissions and restrictions, of rules, regulations, and reporting requirements arising from minor federal reforms and from activities of the individual states. The number of these activities make banking the most highly regulated industry in the country. The regulatory diversity results in banks in each of the states of the union holding a slightly different competitive position with respect to banks in other states and with respect to other financial institutions within their own. Thus, the economic concentration in the hands of the few largest banks, the ability to establish branches, the ability to merge with another financial institution, and in general, the entire structure of the industry varies from state to state.

Competition and Services

The banking industry has never had a monopoly on providing financial services. Through the years, other firms, sensing opportunity for competition in some specific financial market served by the "full service banks," have been established. A partial listing of institutions which at one time or another have performed services closely related to aspects of banking includes the following:

Mutual Savings Banks
Stock Savings Banks
Guaranty Savings Banks
Safe Deposit Companies
Postal Savings System
Investment Banks
Trust Companies
Insurance Underwriting Companies
Mortgage Companies
Savings and Loan Associations (State and Federal)
Rural Electrification Administration, Commodity Credit Corporation, Federal Housing Administration, and other loan activities of the Government
Granger Banks
Consumer Finance Companies
Sales Finance Companies
Manufacturers' Finance Corporations
Credit Unions
Morris Plan Banks
Remedial Loan Societies [4]

Not all of these institutions continue to exist, and those which do have neither the power, the prestige, nor the versatility of the commercial banks. But they all perform services which could be or have been performed by the commercial banks exclusively. In addition, more and more corporations are becoming sophisticated in the use of cash, and are finding ways to use it for productive purposes even over short periods such as weekends rather than allowing it to lie fallow. In recent years, many members of the banking industry have been seeking ways to recapture some of the business lost to these competing institutions, and have also sought new markets through service diversification. This has led to considerable augmentation of the traditional deposit, loan, savings, and exchange services offered by commercial banks. Through increased branching, where it is permitted by state laws, banks have protected their image as "retailers of finance," and have followed the customers to their

---

[4] Herbert Spero, *Money and Banking*, 2nd ed. (New York: Barnes & Noble, Inc., 1953), pp. 153-228.

homes in the suburbs. "Drive-in" windows have been provided
for the customers' convenience. Credit cards, "special" checking
accounts, specialized saving plans, and a variety of new personal
trust services have all been instituted.

Many of these new services have been made possible only
through increased attention to detail, which has required increased mechanization through computers or specialized bookkeeping machinery. The overall result has been vastly increased
demand for clerical personnel in the home-office location, a
factor which has provided many new job opportunities for
Negroes

STRUCTURE OF THE INDUSTRY

The structure of the banking industry is characterized by both
decentralization and concentration. It is a highly dispersed industry, but one which is numerically dominated by a few large
firms.

Concentration

On June 29, 1968, there were 13,683 commercial banks operating in the United States. Although the number of separate
banking organizations makes this country's banking structure
unique, a surprisingly large percentage of the banking business
is conducted in a relatively small number of institutions. The
median bank in the country has something on the order of
$5,000,000 in deposits, but there are ten banks each of whose
deposits are more than 1,000 times greater than this. Those
ten banks are shown in Table 1.

The assets of all commercial banks were $456,827,000,000
at the end of June 1968. Approximately 45 percent of those
assets were in the hands of the fifty largest banks, and about
25 percent of the total assets were in the hands of the top
ten banks. Among the top fifty banks, assets per employee
averaged some three-quarters of a million dollars, and earnings
per employee were over $5,000.[5]

The distribution of commercial banks by size of deposit is
shown in Figure 1. It can be seen from the figure that the
greatest number of banking institutions in the country hold be-

---

[5] Assets per employee were approximately half a million dollars for the
industry as a whole in 1968.

TABLE 1. *The Ten Largest Commercial Banks 1968*

Rank by Assets	Bank	Assets	Deposits	Earnings	Employees	Assets per Employee (Thousands of dollars)	Earnings per Employee (Dollars)
		(Thousands of dollars)					
1	Bank of America (San Francisco)	23,961,437	21,502,892	146,162	32,340	741	4,520
2	First National City Bank (New York)	19,355,215	16,643,247	124,789	30,200	641	4,132
3	Chase Manhattan Bank (New York)	19,014,284	16,709,926	119,480	20,688	919	5,775
4	Manufacturers Hanover Trust (New York)	10,439,165	9,202,392	68,531	11,202	932	6,118
5	Morgan Guaranty Trust of New York	10,369,966	8,211,716	78,100	7,004	1,481	11,151
6	Chemical Bank New York Trust	8,967,729	7,640,535	67,258	11,049	812	6,087
7	Bankers Trust (New York)	7,652,980	6,827,713	52,071	9,426	812	5,524
8	Continental Illinois National Bank and Trust (Chicago)	7,373,394	6,301,503	55,918	6,918	1,066	8,083
9	First National Bank of Chicago	6,530,070	5,746,162	50,814	4,718	1,384	10,770
10	Security Pacific National Bank (Los Angeles)	6,288,197	5,711,376	50,549	13,015	483	3,884
	Total or average: ten largest banks	119,952,437	103,897,462	813,672	146,560	818	5,552
	Total or average: fifty largest banks	209,392,282	181,547,992	1,469,439	278,428	752	5,278

Source: *Fortune,* Vol. LXXIX (May 15, 1969), pp. 190-191.

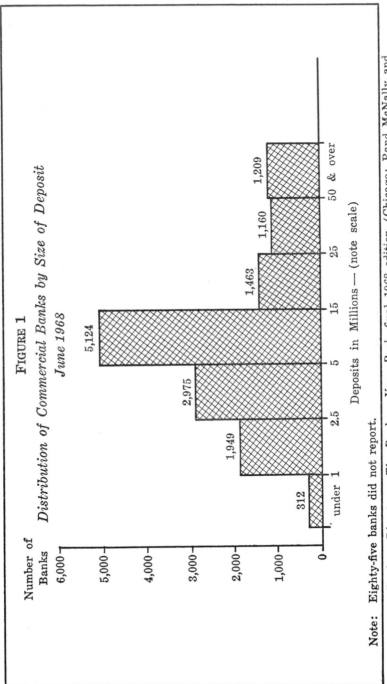

FIGURE 1

Distribution of Commercial Banks by Size of Deposit

June 1968

Number of Banks

Deposits in Millions — (note scale)

Note: Eighty-five banks did not report.

Source: *Bankers Directory: The Bankers Year Book,* final 1968 edition (Chicago: Rand McNally and Company, 1968), p. 72.

tween $5 and $15 million in deposits, and that less than 10 percent of the total hold $50 million or more. With some arithmetic in Figure 1 comparing the deposits to the total shown in Table 1, it can be demonstrated that *the largest ten banks in the country control deposits equal to the aggregate of about the 10,000 smallest banks,* and the fifty largest banks in the country control deposits equivalent to the aggregate of the smallest 13,000.

The institutions classified as "banks" in the country are either commercial banks or stock savings banks. At the end of 1968, there were also 500 mutual savings banks which controlled more than $64 billion in deposits—making them very substantial institutions, indeed, when compared with the average commercial bank. The mutual savings banks are state-chartered and located almost exclusively in the Northeastern portion of the country. (Because of their concentrated location and because their deposit structures are not reflected by large employment structures, the mutual savings banks have been largely neglected in this study.)

Fewer than half (42.2 percent) of the commercial banks in the country are members of the Federal Reserve System. Generally speaking, however, these are the larger banks, and as a result, they control eight-tenths of the total commercial bank deposits. Almost all banks, whether members of the Federal Reserve or not, are insured through the Federal Deposit Insur-

TABLE 2. *Number of Banks by Type of Operation 1941-1968*

December 31	All	Commercial	Mutual Savings	Member	Non-insured
1941	14,826	14,278	548	6,619	852
1945	14,553	14,011	542	6,884	714
1947	14,714	14,181	533	6,923	783
1966	14,271	13,767	504	6,150	233
1967	14,223	13,722	501	6,071	211
1968	14,183	13,683	500	5,981	211ᵃ
Deposits in Millions of Dollars					
1968	496,070	431,820	64,250	354,928	2,438ᵃ

Source: *Federal Reserve Bulletin*, January 1969, pp. A19, A21.
ᵃ As of June 29, 1968.

ance Corporation. As of the end of June 1968, only 211 banks, or 1.5 percent of the total number were uninsured. Generally speaking, these are smaller banks, and they control only 0.5 percent of the deposits of the industry. These relationships are shown in Table 2.

The commercial banks participating in the survey which are part of this study are listed in Appendix A. They are all large banks, and the combined assets of the forty-seven firms listed ($153,140,000,000) are almost exactly one-third of the total assets of all commercial banks.

Decentralization

Despite the high degree of business concentration seen in the above section, the commercial banking structure in the United States exhibits a higher degree of decentralization than that of any other nation.

> Most economically developed countries have banking systems dominated by a few very large institutions with numerous branch offices. In England and Wales, for example, nearly all the domestic banking business is in the hands of eleven branch banks, and over 85 percent is carried on by the "Big Five"—the Midland, the Westminster, Barclays, Lloyds, and the National Provincial—with much of the remainder done by two smaller branch systems. In Canada there were only nine banks in 1958, operating a total of 4,556 domestic banking offices. In the United States, on the other hand, the "unit" or single office bank is still predominant despite the great increase in branch banking, particularly since World War II.[6]

At the end of 1968, of a reported 13,679 (see Table 3) commercial banks in the United States, 9,733 were unit institutions and 3,946 were branch banks (i.e., banks operating more than one office). These 3,946 branch banks conducted business at a total of 18,777 branches, so that while fewer than one-third of the banks in the country were branch banks, two-thirds of the 28,510 banking offices were operated by these multiple office banks.

---

[6] Whittlesey, Freedman, and Herman, *op. cit.*, p. 80.

TABLE 3. *The Commercial Banking Industry*
Banks and Branches by State and Branches by Type of Location Within Each State
1968

State	Commercial Banks (Including Mutual Savings Banks)	Branch Banks[a]	Branches	Branches			
				Located in head office city	Located in head office county	Located in counties contiguous to head office county	Located elsewhere in the state[b]
United States[c]	14,179[d]	3,946	19,675	7,295	6,253	2,940	3,187
Alabama	268	76	230	122	87	10	11
Arizona	13	7	273	92	63	72	46
Arkansas	248	72	140	80	54	5	1
California	162	130	2,751	399	380	567	1,405
Colorado	257	2	2	2	—	—	—
Connecticut	135	86	500	142	275	62	21
Delaware	21	11	88	14	43	27	4
District of Columbia	14	13	97	97	—	—	—
Florida	461	6	6	6	—	—	—
Georgia	428	85	235	174	4	8	49
Idaho	26	14	141	12	13	26	90
Illinois	1,074	39	39	39	—	—	—
Indiana	419	188	573	302	271	48	—
Iowa	673	210	281	97	136	—	—
Kansas	601	59	59	58	1	—	—
Kentucky	346	125	285	175	105	5	—
Louisiana	229	114	327	201	117	6	3
Maine	75	44	217	46	84	75	12
Maryland	128	77	501	147	120	145	89
Massachusetts	332	209	881	428	444	8	1

TABLE 3. *(Continued)*

State	Commercial Banks (Including Mutual Savings Banks)	Branch Banks[a]	Branches	Branches			
				Located in head office city	Located in head office county	Located in counties contiguous to head office county	Located elsewhere in the state[b]
Michigan	338	191	1,095	501	389	194	11
Minnesota	724	6	10	10	—	—	—
Mississippi	185	102	293	125	93	44	31
Missouri	667	83	83	83	—	—	—
Montana	135	3	3	2	—	1	—
Nebraska	441	36	36	36	—	—	—
Nevada	9	7	76	20	17	11	28
New Hampshire	109	37	50	23	23	4	—
New Jersey	250	186	822	284	537	1	—
New Mexico	63	43	112	63	40	8	1
New York	444	271	2,492	1,228	716	454	94
North Carolina	121	75	931	149	97	186	499
North Dakota	169	49	67	9	36	21	1
Ohio	526	261	1,128	513	599	16	—
Oklahoma	424	50	51	51	—	—	—
Oregon	51	29	307	60	44	45	158
Pennsylvania	516	245	1,593	456	648	488	1
Rhode Island	20	20	209	56	89	39	25
South Carolina	118	67	344	83	55	49	157
South Dakota	165	39	91	14	31	23	23

TABLE 3. (Continued)

State	Commercial Banks (Including Mutual Savings Banks)	Branch Banks[a]	Branches				
			Branches	Located in head office city	Located in head office county	Located in counties contiguous to head office county	Located elsewhere in the state[b]
Tennessee	303	131	412	259	138	7	8
Texas	1,151	41	42	42	—	—	—
Utah	54	19	112	23	38	9	42
Vermont	51	25	73	11	27	26	9
Virginia	237	149	694	271	115	135	173
Washington	101	54	524	182	130	72	140
West Virginia	195	4	4	4	—	—	—
Wisconsin	606	139	222	45	141	35	1
Wyoming	70	—	—	—	—	—	—

Source: *Federal Reserve Bulletin*, April 1959, pp. A-91-A-92.

ᵃ A "branch bank" is one which operates two or more offices.

ᵇ In almost all cases, the branching activities of a bank are confined to the state in which the main office is located. However, one New Jersey, one California, one New York, and two Puerto Rican banks operate a total of fourteen branches in other states. The branches are recorded in the states in which they themselves are located.

ᶜ Banks and branches in Alaska, Hawaii, and the Virgin Islands are included in the totals but not in the listings.

ᵈ There is a small discrepancy between the total number of banks shown here and those noted for the same date by other Federal Reserve Board statistics.

Branch banking is a phenomenon of this century. In 1900, there were only 119 branch offices, accounting for less than 1 percent of the total commercial banking offices. At the time, most of the states prohibited the establishment of branch offices. The State of California, in 1909, was the first to relax the legislative and regulatory restraints on branching, but most other states did not follow suit until the 1920's and 1930's. Only thirty-three new branches were opened in the United States in 1938. One hundred and eighty-nine were opened in 1948; 645 were opened in 1958; and it is estimated that over 1,200 were opened in 1968.[7]

A few states, such as Colorado, Florida, Illinois, Texas, West Virginia, and Wyoming still prohibit branch banking, and allow multiple offices only in the event of mergers or in other specified situations. Some states allow branching only in the head office city; some only in the head office county. A few states permit branching in the home office county and in all contiguous counties, and about half of the states permit statewide branching under various restrictions.

A listing of the distribution of banks by state and by the number of branches operating in each state is included as Table 3. (There are some other variations on branching besides those seen in the table. Michigan, for example, allows branching, under some circumstances, into an area formed by a twenty-five mile radius from the home office. Similarly, Virginia allows branching into a five mile radius from the city limits of the city of the home office.)

The banks in Appendix A, which were comprised in our survey, are in locations reflecting seven different degrees of permissiveness toward banking. Eight of the forty-seven are allowed no branches. On the other extreme, one bank alone, the Bank of America, has almost 1,000 branches throughout the State of California. In total, the thirty-nine banks which are allowed branches operate approximately 4,300 of them.

Table 3 also makes clear the great diversity in the number of banking offices located in the various states. Only nine banks, with seventy-six branches, operate in the State of Nevada. At the opposite end of the spectrum is California, with 162 banks operating 2,751 branches. New York is close behind, with a greater number of banks, but fewer branches—319 banks and

---

[7] *Ibid.*, p. 536.

2,205 branches. Texas and Illinois, with 1,151 and 1,074 banks respectively, are the two largest in terms of the number of separate firms. Arizona, Delaware, the District of Columbia, Nevada, and Rhode Island all have fewer than twenty banks. All told, the differences in the number of banking institutions is partially a function of geography, partially of population, and partially of regulation.

Although the total number of banks and branches is large, so is the number of communities which require the services of banks. As a result, many of the smaller unit banks face very little in the way of competition. In the late 1950's, about 60 percent of all unit banks were located in a community with only a single banking office. Eighty-four percent were in communities with only one or two, and only 5 percent operated in areas with competition from more than eight offices.[8]

MANPOWER

In employment, as well as in business and in asset growth, the finance industry has shown more relative growth in the past ten years than any other industrial group except a few service industries and state and local government.

Bank employees work mainly in the densely populated states of New York, California, Pennsylvania, and Illinois, which have the greatest amount of banking services. New York City, the financial capital of the nation, has far more bank employees than any other city. Banking employment is also concentrated, to a considerable extent, in a relatively limited number of large banks and their branches. The top three hundred commercial banks in the country have more than one-half of all commercial bank employees.[9] The 10,000 smallest commercial banks of the country employ an average of about seventy employees each, and the median bank employs about thirteen persons.

Overall employment trends in commercial banking and in the entire financial group, including insurance and real estate, are shown in Table 4. The rapid employment growth can be easily seen in the table. The fact of this growth and the concentration of it in populous areas and large institutions have been factors

---

[8] *Ibid.*, p. 540.

[9] U.S. Bureau of Labor Statistics, *Occupational Outlook Handbook*, 1966-67 ed., p. 612.

TABLE 4.   *Total Employment in Banks and in the Financial Industry*
United States, 1963-1968

Employment	Year					
	1963	1964	1965	1966	1967	1968
Banks (SIC-602)	740,600	766,500	792,000	825,200	868,300	911,300
Finance, insurance, and real estate (SIC-60)	2,877,000	2,957,000	3,023,000	3,100,000	3,217,000	3,357,000

Source: U. S. Bureau of Labor Statistics, *Employment and Earnings Statistics for the United States, 1909-68*, Bulletin No. 1312-6 and *Employment and Earnings*, March 1969.

Note: Includes Alaska and Hawaii beginning 1959.

in creating a favorable climate for the introduction of Negro personnel in the industry.

Commercial banks process more than fifteen billion checks every year, and the number of deposit slips, monthly statements, account clearing sheets, and other paperwork related to the primary function is almost inestimable. Therefore, the banking demand for clerical employees is very high. About two-thirds of all banking employees are in this category. In addition to clerks, machine operators, clerk-typists, secretaries, file clerks, and stenographers, banking also includes thousands of jobs which are unique to banks—the teller jobs—which are also listed in the clerical category. The second largest occupational category in banking is that of officials and managers. Some 18 percent—approximately one in six—of the jobs in the industry are on this level. Professional employees—accountants, lawyers, statisticians, and economists—are the third largest occupational grouping.

Blue collar employees, including guards, porters, elevator operators, and various maintenance and service workers, compose a very small part, less than 5 percent, of total employment. We shall see that this skill mix has had significant effect on Negro employment.

The great bulk of jobs in the banking industry are jobs which require numerical manipulations rather than finger dexterity or physical strength, and as a result are jobs which evidence no particular demand for any specific physical characteristics or strengths of either male or female employees. Especially since the Second World War, banks have been turning increasingly to female employees. Women now make up almost five-eighths of all banking employment, and the proportion of females in the work force continues to rise. The occupational and sex distribution of employees for forty-six of the banks listed in Appendix A is shown in Table 5.

Nature of Work

Because of the overwhelming importance of these jobs as the entry level for employment in banking, it will be instructive to examine the nature of the work of the teller and clerical jobs specific to banking. The following listing is taken, in slightly condensed form, from the Bureau of Labor Statistics occupational outlook report series on banking.[10]

---

[10] U.S. Bureau of Labor Statistics, *Occupational Outlook Handbook*, 1966-67 ed., pp. 614-617.

TABLE 5. *The Banking Industry*
Employment by Sex and Occupational Group
46 Commercial Banks Surveyed
United States, 1968

Occupational Group	Total	Percent	Male	Female
Officials and managers	38,195	18.6	32,931	5,264
Professionals	7,073	3.4	5,533	1,540
Technicians	2,790	1.3	2,336	454
Sales workers	767	0.4	631	136
Office and clerical	147,921	72.0	32,835	115,086
Total white collar	196,746	95.7	74,266	122,480
Craftsmen	767	0.4	731	36
Operatives	1,924	0.9	1,510	414
Laborers and service workers	6,104	3.0	4,851	1,253
Total blue collar	8,795	4.3	7,092	1,703
Total	205,541	100.0	81,358	124,183

Source: Data in the author's possession.

Bank clerks handle the paperwork associated with depositors' checking and savings accounts, loans to individual and business firms, and other bank business. Bank clerks known as *sorters* separate checks, deposit slips, and other bank documents, and tabulate them so that they may be charged to the proper accounts; often they use cancelling and adding machines in their work. *Proof machine operators* use special equipment that sorts items and adds and records the amounts of money involved.

Bookkeeping workers, composing one of the largest segments of the clerical grouping, operate posting machinery especially designed for bank use. By and large, their jobs consist of routine typing, calculating, and posting related to banking transactions. Some of the job titles in this group are: *bookkeeping machine operator, account clerk, posting machine operator, recording clerk, Christmas club bookkeeper, discount bookkeeper, interest accrual bookkeeper, trust bookkeeper, commodity loan clerk, bookkeeping and accounting clerk, reconcilement clerk*, and *trust investment clerk*.

Country collection clerks sort the thousands of pieces of mail that come in daily to the city banks and determine which items must be held at the main office and which should be routed to branch banks or to out-of-city banks for collection. *Transit clerks* perform a variation on this job which consists of sorting bank items such as drafts on other banks, and preparing the documents so that they can be mailed for collection.

Exchange clerks service foreign deposit accounts. *Interest clerks* and *mortgage clerks* maintain records relating to interest bearing items.

As of the end of 1964, approximately 700 banks had already installed electronic data processing equipment. Many new jobs, unique to banks, have grown from the use of this equipment, including those of the *electronic reader-sorter operator* who operates electronic check-sorting equipment, the *check inscriber* or *encoder* who operates the machinery that prints information on checks in magnetic ink, and the *control clerk* who keeps track of the large volume of documents flowing in and out of the computer division. This has been an important source of jobs for Negroes.

Commercial tellers, with whom most people deal when they transact business in banks, are mainly occupied with cashing customers' checks and handling deposits and withdrawals from checking and savings accounts during the hours that the bank is open to the public. The duties of the job include verifying the identity of persons to whom payments are to be made, ascertaining that funds are in the accounts against which checks are drawn, checking to see whether deposit slips are correctly itemized, entering passbook or deposit receipt totals, and using a variety of special posting machinery. After public banking hours, the teller is responsible for counting cash on hand, listing currency received, and balancing the daily accounts. Other incidental tasks include sorting checks and deposit slips, filing new account cards, and removing closed account cards from files.

The functions of other teller positions are similar, although they may have special titles such as *savings, foreign exchange, payroll, discount,* or *securities tellers.*

Special Requirements

For the clerical positions, high school graduation is generally considered adequate preparation for beginning jobs. For most of them, courses in bookkeeping, typing, or business arithmetic are desirable. In addition, to these requirements, in the hiring of tellers, employers prefer experience in some related clerical

position. They also pay strict attention to personal characteristics such as neatness, tact, and courtesy. These are particularly important because customers, who deal with tellers far
more frequently than with any other bank employees, often
judge a bank's services principally on their impression of the
teller. We shall see that these factors were long a deterrent to
hiring Negroes for teller positions.

Since tellers handle large amounts of money, they must be
able to meet the standards established by bonding companies.

Banking wages for either clerical positions or teller positions
are not particularly high, and are generally less than or equivalent to clerical positions in manufacturing or government.
Nevertheless, wages have been increasing rapidly from year to
year.

Union Affiliation

Banks have entered into very few collective bargaining agree-
ments with their employees. Despite the recent unionization of
one small, New Jersey bank, and the apparently successful strike
called by a banking union in Seattle, there is no indication that
union activities or unionization in the banking industry is in-
tensifying or becoming anymore common.[11]

EFFECT OF BANKING STRUCTURE ON NEGRO
EMPLOYMENT

The aspects of the structure of the American banking industry
which were chosen for discussion in this chapter are all factors
which will be seen in subsequent discussions to have an effect
on the levels of Negro employment found in the industry.

The highly varied industrial location and structure resulting
from regulations affecting the average size of banks, from decentralization, from branching, and from other causes, and the
degree of concentration which locates most of the industry's
employment in a few large banks in a few large cities have an

---

[11] *Wall Street Journal*, January 2, 1968, p. 1. (Four of the banks surveyed
by the author did report some recent union overtures to their employees, but
none developed beyond the "probing" stage.) In a decision announced on
November 7, 1969, the National Labor Relations Board ruled that a single
branch of a bank was an "appropriate unit" for collective bargaining. Since
it is easier to unionize one branch than a large grouping, this decision was
obviously designed to encourage bank unionization. (*Matter of Wells Fargo
Bank*, 179 NLRB No. 79, November 7, 1969.)

obvious effect on the jobs offered by the industry and the population available to accept them. Diversification of services and rapid employment growth have insured that jobs have been available.

The initial instability of the industry, its historical importance as a source of both credit and crisis, its unionization structure, its prestige status, and the general character of its work requirements all affect the image of the industry to Negroes, as a more or a less desirable place to seek employment. The white collar orientation of the industry, the high skill levels required for even entry-level jobs, its increasingly female orientation, and factors growing from services of the industry such as the handling of cash and important documents, all affect Negro employment levels. The evolution of these employment levels will be described and analyzed in the chapters which follow.

CHAPTER III

Negro Employment Levels:
National Data, 1940-1968

Until the pattern began to crumble at about the time of the First World War, the banking industry generally eschewed the business as well as the employment of Negroes and most other minority group members. This practice caused the growth through the years of "Granger banks and labor banks, industrial banks and immigrant banks, Hibernian, Germanian, and Scandinavian banks, and a wide variety of styles of private banks. When a group of bank customers felt themselves inadequately served, the way was usually open to start a new bank." [12] (A large number of Negro banks were also founded. See Appendix B.)

As economically-oriented institutions, banks soon enough gave way to the demands for their services by all minority groups; but it is only in the very recent past that minority group members of any sort, and particularly Negroes, were accepted as employees actively participating in the affairs of the organizations.

THE 1940-1960 ERA

During the twenty years from 1940 to 1960, the financial industry was characterized by rapid employment growth—almost three times the rate of all private industry. Of the 475,660 employees in the industry in 1940, only 7,294, or 1.5 percent, were Negro. Twenty years later, in 1960, Negro employment had more than doubled to 19,572. But total employment had more than doubled—to 1,018,046—so that Negroes still composed less than 2 percent of the total work force.

Comparing these Negro employment figures with those for all industry (including agriculture), we find that all industry employed proportionally four times more Negroes than the financial community, and at over 9 percent Negro in their work forces, came much closer to approximating the 10-11 percent

---

[12] Paul B. Trescott, *Financing American Enterprise* (New York: Harper & Row, 1963), p. 268.

Negro population proportion which existed during this period. These statistics are found in Table 6.

Included in the "banking" category as defined by the Bureau of Census were all of the savings and loan associations and various other financial institutions in addition to banks. Also included were the (approximately) seven all-Negro banks and several dozen Negro savings and loan associations. (Fifty Negro savings and loan existed in 1938, of which twenty-two remained in business in 1947.) The number of Negro institutions was not great, and all of them were small. (They are discussed in Appendix B.) Still, discounting their several hundred employees from the already small total number of Negroes in the financial community, and considering that there were well over ten thousand each of commercial banks and savings and loan associations, we see that there remained considerably fewer than one Negro per banking establishment, even in 1960.

During this twenty-year span, the employment composition in banking was shifting rapidly, but it was not particularly a racial shift—rather one of male-female composition. The table shows that females, who were less than one-third of employment prior to World War II, were more than a majority by 1960. Among Negroes, the female employment proportion increased more rapidly than male, and this probably indicates that the traditional jobs held by Negroes in the industry, such as the male-oriented service and maintenance jobs, were giving way in some small degree to female-oriented clerical positions.

EMPLOYMENT CHANGES, 1960-1966

Substantial changes in the racial composition of banking work forces apparently began to take place in the early 1960's. Measurement of the extent of those changes, however, is very difficult prior to 1966. In a few specific areas, where active human relations agencies functioned, data can be found, and we shall present the experiences of banks in several cities in which this was the case in Chapter VI.

In many other areas, however, banks were prohibited by state laws from maintaining records of the racial characteristics of their work forces. For this reason, or from the lack of desire to do so, many banks did not produce statistical reports of the race of their employees until required to do so by federal law in 1966. Thus, extensive data on a national scale are not available for his-

TABLE 6.   The Banking Industry Compared With All Industries
Employment by Race and Sex, United States, 1940-1960

	Total			Male			Female		
	1940	1950	1960	1940	1950	1960	1940	1950	1960
BANKING[a]									
Employment	475,660	516,240	1,018,046	329,664	261,720	473,771	145,996	254,520	544,275
Negro	7,294	9,300	19,572	6,322	6,780	12,046	972	2,520	7,526
Other racial minorities	351	420	6,236	280	150	2,585	71	270	3,651
Percent									
Negro	1.5	1.8	1.9	1.9	2.6	2.5	0.7	1.0	1.4
All female	30.7	49.3	53.5	—	—	—	—	—	—
Negro female	13.3	27.1	38.5	—	—	—	—	—	—
ALL INDUSTRIES									
Employment	45,166,083	55,813,380	64,639,256	34,027,905	40,060,560	43,466,955	11,138,178	15,752,820	21,172,301
Negro	4,479,068	5,385,900	6,099,089	2,936,795	3,499740	3,643,949	1,542,273	1,886,160	2,455,140
Other racial minorities	191,926	230,460	529,901	159,604	179,040	361,317	32,322	51,420	168,584
Percent									
Negro	9.9	9.6	9.4	8.6	8.7	8.4	13.8	12.0	11.6
All female	24.7	28.2	32.8	—	—	—	—	—	—
Negro female	34.4	35.0	40.3	—	—	—	—	—	—

Source: *U.S. Census of Population:*

    1940:   Vol. III, *The Labor Force*, Part 1, Table 18.
    1950:   P-E No. 1D, *Industrial Characteristics*, Table 2.
    1960:   Vol. I, *Industrial Characteristics*, Part D, Table 213, 214.
    [a] Includes savings and loan associations and various other financial institutions.

torical comparison or for illustrating the details of changes in the industry.

Nevertheless, a small field sample of six banks from across the country was taken in 1964. Although not national in scope, it is of sufficient interest to be discussed here. The survey revealed that among 48,250 employees covered, a total of just under 1,400, or 2.9 percent, were Negro. To the extent that these banks were representative of the entire industry, the figures would indicate a modest improvement over the 1960 census results.

Without dwelling on the figures themselves in this small survey, we would like to point out one factor of importance relative to the structure of the banking industry. In these survey banks, 12.1 percent of all blue collar workers were Negro; 2.7 percent of the white collar workers were Negro. Yet the weighted average shows that only 2.9 percent of all workers were Negro. Thus, the relatively high proportion of Negroes among blue collar employees has changed the weighted average by only two-tenths of one percentage point, indicating that blue collar employment is not very important in the industry and that the Negro proportion in blue collar jobs is neither critical nor an adequate indicator of the overall employment pattern.

Another point which bears mentioning takes the form of a caveat against any overly literal interpretation of statistics by occupational grouping in any year.[13] Of the six firms surveyed, two reported no blue collar employees at all. Of the remaining four—all of them large and of about the same size—one showed no professional employees, a different one, no technicians. Only one of the six reported employing craftsmen, and the number of operatives varied from none to 367. Five of these are commercial banks of a similar nature and size, and have similar personnel requirements and job titles; but it would be impossible to say so from their occupational statistics. It is for this reason that little emphasis will be placed on job categories subsequently in this study.

1966 DATA

In the Spring of 1966, all commercial banks with one hundred or more employees were required to file a report on the racial

---

[13] The standard occupational groupings used by banks and other firms in recording their Negro employment patterns follows. In the white collar group are: officials and managers, professionals, technicians, sales workers, and office and clerical workers. In the blue collar group are: craftsmen, operatives, laborers, and service workers.

composition of their work forces with the Equal Employment
Opportunity Commission (EEOC), which had been established by
Title VII of the Civil Rights Act of 1964. (For the legislative
history and the evolution of reporting requirements by banks, see
Appendix C.) Because of this reporting requirement, almost all
of the larger banks in the country began to keep such records,
and as a result, broad-based statistical data are available. The
results of a field sample of 738 commercial banks will be presented shortly. First, however, there is a source of difficulty involving the dating of statistical reports which requires clarifica-
tion if future problems are to be avoided.

Dating of Reports

When the government reporting requirements were established,
banks were instructed to submit in March of 1966 data collected
at the end of the previous December, January, or February. The
Equal Employment Opportunity Commission and other government agencies have always referred to the data thus collected as
"1966 data." The author has maintained, and continues to maintain, that these data are much more representative of the policies,
procedures, and employment practices of the individual firms during 1965 than 1966, which was a maximum of two months old
when the numbers were taken.

The government numbering procedure has the effect of retarding apparent hiring improvement, or any other changes, by one
year, and has caused much needless confusion within the banking
industry and elsewhere. Nevertheless, because we shall be comparing field sample data with published government reports, we
feel we would complicate an already complex situation yet further
by failing to be consistent. We shall, therefore, follow the government numbering procedure.

EEOC Data, 1966

Early in 1969, the Equal Employment Opportunity Commission
made public the statistical compilations for Negro employment in
all industries for 1966. These are extensive data, and will be
used heavily for a number of comparisons in later sections of this
study.

Summarized totals of employment data for the banking industry, by race and job classification, are shown in Table 7.

TABLE 7.   *The Banking Industry*
Employment by Race and Occupational Group
United States, 1966

Occupational Group	Total	Negro	Percent Negro
Officials and managers	88,107	343	0.4
Professionals	10,787	83	0.8
Technicians	3,811	243	6.4
Sales workers	2,648	13	0.5
Office and clerical	373,251	14,080	3.8
Total white collar	478,604	14,762	3.1
Total blue collar	32,271	7,819	24.2
Total	510,875	22,581	4.4

Source: U. S. Equal Employment Opportunity Comission, *Job Patterns for Minorities and Women in Private Industry-1966*, Report No. 1, Part II (Washington: The Commission, 1968).

The results from this table can be compared with the 1960 census data seen in Table 6.   The rise in the proportion of Negroes employed is most spectacular.   In 1966, Negroes were 4.4 percent of total banking employment, up from 1.9 percent in 1960.   During this period, the banking industry was continuing to expand in total employment, so that the proportion of Negroes hired was considerably greater than 4.4 percent.[14]

Field Sample Data, 1966

As a complement to the published EEOC data, additional information for 1966 is available from a field sample of some 738 indi-

---

[14] If a firm is expanding and its Negro participation ratio remains the same, then its hiring rate of Negroes is in the same proportion, thus:

A firm of 1,000 employees, 2% black, has 20 Negroes. If it expands by 10%, it will have 1,100 employees. With the same (2%) participation ratio, it will now have 22 Negroes. One hundred new employees were added, 2 of the 100 were Negroes, and hiring proportion remains at 2%.

However:

A firm of 1,000 employees, 2% black, has 20 Negroes. If it expands by 10%, it will have 1,100 employees. With a higher participation ratio (say 5%), it will have now 55 Negroes. One hundred new employees were added, 35 of the 100 were Negroes, and the hiring proportion is 35%.

vidual commercial banks. Although not as complete in coverage of the industry, these data are in different form than the EEOC report, and allow certain state and regional breakdowns, evaluation of employment patterns in insitutions of different sizes, and other statistical accumulations which are not possible from the published data.

When field sample data are duplicated by figures from the published EEOC report, we shall use the latter. Nevertheless, to illustrate the extensiveness of the field sample and to show the high degree of similarity of results between the two sets of figures, a compendium of the sample results has been included as Table 8.

Female employment which appears in Table 8 can be compared with earlier figures from Table 6. The trend toward increasingly female banking work forces which began in 1940 can be seen as continuing through 1966, when 57 percent of all employment in the industry was female.

The table also shows that although two of every three Negroes employed are in white collar jobs, more than nine out of every ten persons in the industry are in white collar jobs, and the Negro employment rate for these jobs is therefore considerably less than that for other races.

RECENT DEVELOPMENT AND TRENDS, 1967 AND 1968

Data on hand and revised as of March 1969 covering banking employment for 1967 and 1968 are drawn from a somewhat different population of banks than are earlier statistics. As has been mentioned, the 1966 statistics were taken from banks subject to the nondiscrimination provisions of the Civil Rights Act of 1964, which included firms with more than one hundred employees. Subsequent to August 1966, however, all banks holding deposits of the United States Government (regardless of the size of deposit) were deemed to be contractors to the government and therefore subject to the President's executive order 11246 prohibiting discrimination.[15] Under the provisions of this order, all banks with government deposits and with fifty or more employees were required to file reports and maintain records on minority employment. Thus, many additional banks, having between fifty and one hundred employees, began to keep racial statistics and

---

[15] Letter in the author's possession from Henry H. Fowler, Secretary of the Treasury, to "The Chief Executive Officer of the Bank Addressed," Washington, August 1966.

TABLE 8. *The Banking Industry*
Employment by Race, Sex, and Occupational Classification
738 Banks
United States, 1966

All Employees			376,017
White collar			352,428
Male white collar		144,905	
Female white collar		207,523	
White collar as percent of all employees			93.7
All Negro Employees			16,561
Negro white collar			11,011
Male white collar		3,403	
Female white collar		7,608	
Negro white collar as percent of all Negro employees			66.5
Negroes as percent of all employees			4.4
Negro white collar as percent of total white collar			3.1
Total females as percent of all employees			57.0
Female white collar as percent of total white collar			58.9
Negro female white collar as percent of total Negro white collar			69.1

Source: Data in author's possession.

many of these smaller banks were included in the 1967 and 1968 surveys.[16]

As we shall see in Chapter V, there apparently is a direct correlation between size of firm and proportion of Negroes employed. Thus, by including banks with smaller work forces in our surveys, we eliminate some of the upward bias which systematic sampling error may have introduced into the 1966 figures.

Comparable Statistics, *1967* and *1968*

A most interesting sub-set of the 1967 and 1968 data can be drawn from the more complete statistics available. It consists of the figures from about 1,300 individual banks which had information for both 1967 and 1968. This is a sub-set of *comparable* data, and is invaluable for analyzing growth and hiring patterns between the two years.

The picture of change presented is very encouraging. In 1967, the total employment for these banks was 483,348, and their Negro employment 24,436, making 5.1 percent Negro overall. Between 1967 and 1968, total employment grew by 6.1 percent, raising the work force total to 512,714. Simultaneously, the number of Negroes in banks increased by 24.7 percent, to a total Negro employment of 30,483. In 1968, Negroes made up 5.9 percent of all employment in these banks.

An even more optimistic picture is presented if we look at the growth figures specifically. Between 1967 and 1968, the 1,300 banks created 29,366 new jobs. Six thousand and forty-seven of these were filled by Negroes. If we can assume that the turnover rate for Negroes and non-Negroes already employed was approximately the same, then this means that 20.6 percent of all persons added by the industry (for the "1968" report) were Negro. And if the Negro turnover rate were actually greater than that for non-Negroes, this hiring rate would be even higher.

These data and some similar figures showing the breakdown of the work force by sex are seen in Table 9. Also included in that table are the 1966 data taken from Table 8, which, although not directly comparable to the two subsequent years' figures, are included to illustrate the continuing trends.

---

[16] The average bank in the country in 1968 had 67 employees. See **Tables** 2 and 4 in Chapter II.

TABLE 9. *The Banking Industry*
Employment by Race and Sex
United States, 1966-1968

	1966	1967	1968
Number of Reporting Units	738	1,300	1,300
Total Employment	376,017	483,348	512,714
Total Male	161,705	188,089	196,844
Total Female	214,312	295,259	315,870
Total Negro Employment	16,561	24,436	30,483
Negro Male	N.A.	10,181	11,816
Negro Female	N.A.	14,255	18,667
Percent Negro Employment	4.4	5.1	5.9
Male	N.A.	5.4	6.0
Female	N.A.	4.8	5.9
Percent Growth, 1967-1968			
All Employees		D.N.A.	6.1
Negro Employees		D.N.A.	24.7
Percent of Total Employment			
Growth Made Up by Negroes		D.N.A.	20.6

Source: Table 8 and data in author's possession.

Overall Statistics, *1967* and *1968*

The more complete data, revised as of March 1969, include an additional 200 banks (approximately) which had figures available for 1967 but not 1968, and approximately 400 which had figures available for 1968 but not 1967. Because they represent the results of larger samples, these data, although unsuitable for analysis of growth, are better indications of the overall employment picture in the industry in each of these years.

For 1967, with 1,500 banks reporting, total employment stood at 535,000, Negro employment at 26,000, and the proportion Negro employed at 4.9 percent. (These numbers are all approximations.) For 1968, with 1,700 banks reporting, total employment was recorded at 667,082, and total Negro employment at 37,396, for 5.6 percent Negro. This information is recorded in Table 10.

Comparing the figures from Table 9 with those on Table 10 reveals that the inclusion of additional banks in the revised data resulted in a decrease in the total percentage Negro recorded.

This decrease could be attributed to a number of causes, of which two stand out. First, the average size of the additional four hundred banks is slightly smaller than that of the first 1,300. Second, many of the reports came from banks located in areas of very small Negro population concentration. Some data on minority employment as well as Negro employment are presented in Table 10.

TABLE 10. *The Banking Industry*
Employment by Race and Sex
United States, 1967-1968

	1967	1968
Number of reporting units (approximate)	1500	1700
All Employees	535,000	667,082
Total male	N.A.	285,200
Total female	N.A.	381,882
All Minority Employees	N.A.	60,824
Minority male	N.A.	25,286
Minority female	N.A.	35,538
All Negro Employees	26,000	37,396
Negro male	N.A.	16,637
Negro female	N.A.	20,759
Percent Minority Employment	N.A.	9.1
Male	N.A.	8.9
Female	N.A.	9.3
Percent Negro Employment	4.9	5.6
Male	N.A.	5.8
Female	N.A.	5.4
Negro as percent of all minority employees		61.5

Source: Data in author's possession; revised as of March 1, 1969.

SURVEY DATA, 1968

In the Summer and Fall of 1968, fifty banks in seventeen cities throughout the country were contacted by the author on the subject of their Negro employment. Forty-nine of these were commercial banks. Forty-seven of the forty-nine consented to participate in the survey, and forty-six of the forty-seven provided detailed statistical data as well as responses to more subjective questions. The institutions which participated in these interviews, and a few words about the survey itself, are to be found in Appendix A.

Although the interviews were national in scope, employing the statistics drawn from them requires some care. These are all large banks by comparison with industry averages. Although they constitute only some 2.7 percent of all banks filing reports in 1968, these banks comprise 30 percent of the total reported employment. Therefore some question exists as to how representative they are of the industry as a whole. (The relationship between size of institutions and Negro employment level will be discussed in Chapter V.)

Even if not particularly representative of the industry as a whole, there is a twofold significance attached to these banks. First, the problems with and concern for Negro employment are predominantly a factor in major cities, and these survey banks are located in a cross-section of the largest cities in the country. Their reactions and their handling of methodologies for increasing Negro employment are the ones which count most heavily. Secondly, these forty-six banks employed 45 percent of all of the Negroes reported in the entire industry in 1968. The various statistical breakdowns for this group of banks are shown in Table 11. In 1968, their Negro employment totaled 8.1 percent of the total work force, and Negro white collar workers were 7.6 percent of the white collar group.

OVERALL TRENDS, 1940-1968

The banking industry in this country has not been a traditional place of employment for Negroes, and even on the verge of 1970 it is anything but overwhelming Negro. The overall trend in the numbers and proportions of Negroes in bank work forces, however, is unmistakeably upward. Figure 2 brings together the available data on the Negro population proportion and the proportion of banking employment. The figure makes it clear that there was a considerable change in attitudes in the industry in the early 1960's, resulting in a dramatic increase in the level of Negro employment.

If the rise is dramatic, one of the factors which makes it so is the lack of change in industry hiring patterns prior to that time. The labor market pertubations which affected employment patterns in most industries after 1940 as a result of the manpower

TABLE 11. The Banking Industry

Employment by Race, Sex, and Occupational Classification
46 Commercial Banks Surveyed
United States, 1968

All Employees		205,541
White collar		196,746
Male white collar	74,266	
Female white collar	122,480	
White collar as percent of all employees		95.7
All Negro Employees		16,726
Negro white collar		14,874
Male white collar	3,775	
Female white collar	11,099	
Negro white collar as percent of all Negro employees		88.9
Negroes as percent of all employees		8.1
Negro white collar as percent of total white collar		7.6
Total females as percent of all employees		60.4
Female white collar as percent of total white collar		62.3
Negro female white collar as percent of total Negro white collar		74.6

Source: Data in author's possession.

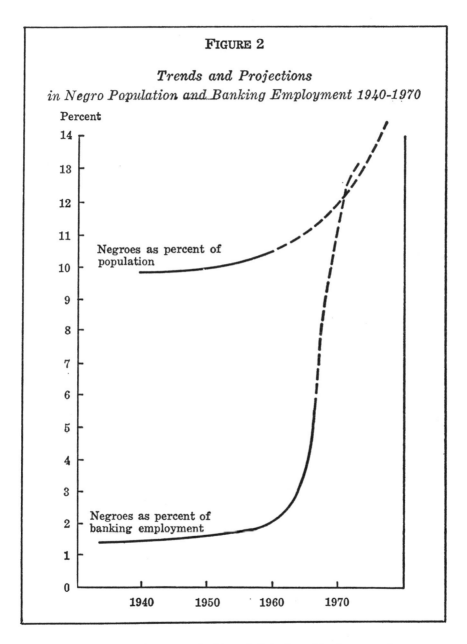

FIGURE 2

Trends and Projections
in Negro Population and Banking Employment 1940-1970

Percent

Negroes as percent of population

Negroes as percent of banking employment

1940   1950   1960   1970

Source: Tables 6, 7, 10, 21, and data in author's possession.

needs growing from the military conscriptions and emphasis on military production were felt by the banking industry, but the shift which came about was in the male-female mix rather than in the racial composition of the work forces. As a result, in racial terms, the industry remained generally more exclusive, less integrated than most by 1960 and had had little previous experience with race issues.

In the 1940 census of the population, reports on the racial composition of eighty-two industrial categories were shown. At that time, compared with the banking group (which included savings and loans, etc.), twelve industries had a smaller proportion of male Negro workers and twenty-two showed relatively fewer female Negroes. In the following twenty years, the racial employment patterns in almost all industries underwent greater change than in banking. In the 1960 census, only three categories, "footwear except rubber," "communications," and "legal, engineering, and miscellaneous professional" still had fewer Negro males; and with a single exception—"mining"—banks employed the lowest proportion of Negro females of any industry.

Thus it was from a very low statistical base that improvement in racial employment began in banking in the early 1960's, and this low base, along with the personnel attitudes which accompanied it, is still very easily recalled by compiance agencies and by qualified Negroes who might otherwise apply to the industry for jobs. Therefore, it is to the detriment of the industry in several ways that it waited so long to embrace equal employment ideas; but in fairness it should be pointed out that there were many factors particular to the banking employment structure which made experimentation with employee patterns seem risky in the eyes of many of the industry's personnel men.

In any event, the level of Negro employment in banking only changed from about 1.5 percent of the work force in 1940 to somewhat less than 2 percent twenty years later, in 1960. After 1960, it increased rapidly, and grew at a rate of just slightly less than a compounded 15 percent per year. The 1968 level was three times that of 1960, and stood at almost 6 percent of the total work force. Projection of the trend illustrated in Figure 2 indicates that banks will be employing Negroes at their population proportion by 1972 or 1973.

Female Advances

Another major trend in banking employment is the status of women in the industry. As mentioned, hiring greater numbers of females was banking's response to wartime labor shortages. During the early 1940's female participation shot up from 30 to 45 percent of the work force. Over the following twenty years, the female employment proportion increased but at a decreasing rate, and probably would have continued a modest increase or stabilized were it not for the sudden increase in clerical work brought about by the introduction of computers, the general spread in the sponsoring of credit cards by banks, and the increased desire for banking services by the general public during the affluent 1960's. These factors made more jobs available for females, and changes in sociological viewpoints during the same time meant that there were more women seeking jobs. The most recent figures show that 57 percent of bank employees are female.

The increase in Negro females as a proportion of total Negro employment started in 1940 at an even lower base, but has changed more rapidly, so that by 1968 their participation ratio was almost identical with the overall female pattern. The Negro female gains are a result of clerical-level hirings, but this is only half the picture. A proper understanding requires realization that the initial low female proportion resulted from the practice of using Negroes, when hired at all, in porter, guard, messenger, maintenance, and miscellaneous service jobs, all of which are male-oriented. Even now, although the female proportion of Negroes is about the same as for non-Negroes, there is a substantive difference in the distribution of the male jobs.

In each job category, the ratio of female to male employees is about the same for Negroes as for non-Negroes. Females of all races are underrepresented in both the high-level—officer and manager, professional, sales, and technical—positions and in blue collar jobs. They are overrepresented in office and clerical jobs. Although the proportion of persons holding office and clerical positions is about the same for Negroes as for non-Negroes, Negroes are overrepresented in the blue collar jobs and underrepresented in the high-level positions compared to non-Negroes. The top jobs are thus predominantly white male, the middle jobs predominantly female, and the blue collar jobs predominantly Negro male.

INDICATIONS FOR 1969

Among personnel men in the forty-seven banks comprised by the survey, none saw any indications that the generally upward trend of Negro representation in banks was coming to an end or even slowing down. And only in a rare case did a bank indicate that its own organization would not change much toward a more heavily Negro racial composition in the near future. One comment representative of this group follows:

> We hired quite a few new people last year when we put in the new credit card. The labor market here is not particularly tight now, so we don't have much trouble getting qualified people this year. There was quite a jump up in Negro hiring last year, but although I don't have the figures, I suspect the rate might be a little lower now.

Comments representative of the more common experience of expanding Negro employment are the following:

> Our hiring went from 25.9 percent last year overall to 41.7 percent in the first quarter of 1968.

> Well, I don't really know [what the hiring rate is] but more than 25 percent of our current applicants are Negro.

> Through May of this year, almost 9 percent of our new hires have been Negroes. This is about three times what it was last year, and doesn't count the NAB program additions.

> We had a 30 percent increase in black hiring last year, and I am sure it will be even more this year.

Finally, and perhaps most typical of all:

> Negro applications and hirings have both doubled in the past five years, and it certainly doesn't look like either is going to be slowing down any.[17]

Interview comments of this sort are not the most positive or persuasive arguments which would be formulated for indicating continued growth in Negro representation in banks; and yet there seems little reason to question them. Those interviewed merely confirm the author's random sampling observations of bank hiring offices: Negroes were present, seeking employment (at least

---

[17] Interviews, various cities, 1968.

during the summer and fall of 1968) in large numbers. By whatever means, the word has apparently spread that employment opportunities are available to Negroes in the major financial institutions.

Perhaps more important, conditions are now much more amenable to the acceptance of Negroes seeking jobs in banking. First, the number of Negroes now generally employed by the average, large, city bank is great enough that the presence of a Negro employee in any department is not a subject of disruptive curiosity. Thus banks are more hospitable to Negroes seeking positions, and the Negroes will be spared the fears of isolation, stares, and other manifestations of close scrutiny attendant to being obviously noticeable in a different (and sometimes hostile) environment.

Second, there is clear evidence that in most such banks, the fears of executives about the internal and external consequences of hiring Negroes, of hiring Negroes for public contact jobs, of promoting Negroes to supervisory positions, of employing Negroes in the personnel function, or using Negroes elsewhere have been largely groundless. These initial deterrents having been overcome, banks are hiring from among the Negro applicants. The indications of this chapter are that the hiring is being done at a rapidly increasing rate.

CONCLUSIONS

The data presented in this chapter have been very carefully selected as the most representative figures available covering the racial employment patterns of the banking industry on a national scale. Systematic statistical errors, where known, have been identified. Nevertheless, the utility of these national data is somewhat limited. It must be remembered that national percentage figures are "average" figures; and in the averaging process, no differentiation can be made between a bank in Lincoln, Nebraska, and one in Jackson, Mississippi. Yet, judging by even superficial analysis, we know from the Negro population proportions of each city that a bank of the same size in each having the national average in Negro employment would be overrepresentative of the Negro population of Lincoln and underrepresentative of it in Jackson. In other words, the national average figures are not a valid standard of comparison for the performance of specific banks.

A second problem concerns the use of averages for performance evaluation at all. Overall trends provide an average against which the performance of an individual bank can be measured, but do not address the question of whether the "normal" pattern is a sufficient one. That question we shall leave to the government agencies charged with evaluating it and to the consensus of individual banking executives. In this study, our focus is to lay before individual bankers as much information as possible about the "normal" pattern for his industry, for his city or area of the country, for institutions the size of his own, etc. By analyzing that pattern, it will be possible to isolate the major factors which seem to have the greatest effect on Negro employment levels. This will be discussed in the ensuing chapters.

CHAPTER IV

Analyzing the Factors Causing Differences Among Industries

The type and quantity of labor demanded or desired by different industries varies with a great number of factors, among them technological and product requirements, job requirements, wage levels, and tradition. The type and quantity of labor supplied or offered to industries is subject to a similar diversity of causes, including wage levels, working conditions, industry image, and perceived welcome. Discrimination and racial bigotry affect demand for minority group members directly and affect supply indirectly through industry image. Let us look more closely at these and related factors as they affect overall employment patterns for Negroes in the banking industry.

JOB REQUIREMENTS, HIGH SKILL

There is no question about the banking industry being very much a white collar industry. In fact, with over 90 percent white collar jobs, it has one of the highest levels in the country of this type of position. Partially, this is required by the particular service offered by the industry, and partially it is a result of a conscious policy to reduce personnel problems in the work force by contracting-out many of the blue collar service requirements such as cafeteria or building maintenance.

The question is does this white collar concentration affect Negro employment, and if so, why? The data on this, while not exhaustive, are consistent enough to give a pretty clear indication that Negro representation decreases with an increasing proportion of white collar positions.

White Collar Comparisons

Table 12 compares banking with all reported employment in the top sixty industries in the country (by employment size) and with the industries which reported the greatest and least proportional Negro representation. The data for this table were drawn from the Equal Employment Opportunity Report (No. 1) which contains the accumulated data from more than 17,500 firms in all industries.[18]

---

[18] U. S. Equal Employment Opportunity Commission, *Job Patterns for Minorities and Women in Private Industry, 1966*, Report No. 1 (Washington: The Commission, 1968), Part I.

41

Obviously, banking was not one of the leaders in Negro employment in 1966. The industry had about 2 percent of all employment, but only about 1 percent of Negro employment. But banks have a more even distribution of Negroes by job classification than is the case in most industries. The top sixty industries in the country are seen to have had 8.2 percent Negro in their overall work force, but only 2.5 percent in the white collar work force. Banking was 4.4 percent overall, but 3.1 percent in the white collar positions. Agriculture, contract construction, and lumber and wood products, among others, each had more than 12 percent Negro overall but less than 1 percent Negro white collar workers.

Figure 3 is drawn from the same source materials as Table 12, and shows the degree of correlation which exists between white collar employment and Negro employment. Looking at the right-hand side of that figure, we can see that there is a fair correlation between increasing levels of white collar employment and decreasing levels of Negro employment in all major industries. Following the statistical trends in this table would lead us to expect less Negro representation in the banking industry than in electronics assembly or automobile repair, or than in the average of all American industries where white collar employment accounts for about half instead of 90 percent of all jobs.

The next question is why this should be the case. There are two general arguments which can be synopsized briefly. On the one hand is the allegation by the Equal Employment Opportunity Commission (and others) to the effect that racial discrimination is more rampant in industries using higher proportions of white collar employees. This certainly is a possible explanation, but it becomes somewhat less persuasive when it is noted, from the left-hand side of Figure 3, that there is also a direct (though not as strong) correlation between an increasing white collar orientation and the proportion of Negroes in white collar jobs. Thus, if it can be said that industries having a large number of white collar jobs discriminate more against Negroes in general, it must also be said that they discriminate relatively less in the higher-ranking jobs, which would seem odd logic on the part of the discriminators.

The second argument comes from those who allege that white collar jobs are more demanding, higher-skilled jobs for which Negroes are less prepared.

TABLE 12.   *Negro Employment in Top Sixty Industries United States, 1966*

Industry	All Employees			White Collar			Blue Collar			Service		
	Total	Negro	Per cent Negro	Total	Negro	Per cent Negro	Total	Negro	Per cent Negro	Total	Negro	Per cent Negro
	Thousands of Employees											
Top 60 Industries	25,594	2,090	8.2	11,004	281	2.5	12,628	1,357	10.7	1,962	452	23.0
	Actual Number of Employees											
Banking	510,875	22,581	4.4	478,604	14,762	3.1	6,947	1,020	14.7	25,324	6,799	26.8
Industry with greatest overall percent Negro (Personal services)	93,809	34,180	36.4	25,129	1,519	6.0	61,433	30,141	49.1	7,247	2,520	34.8
Industry with greatest percent Negro white collar (Medical services)	1,059,794	174,132	16.4	596,032	42,852	7.2	90,429	17,819	19.7	373,333	113,461	30.4
Industry with lowest percent Negro—Overall and white collar (Pipeline transportation)	15,614	75	0.5	6,536	11	0.2	8,998	41	0.5	80	23	28.8
Among these 60 industries in Negro employment, banking ranked, from the top		46			14			26			25	

Source: U.S. Equal Employment Opportunity Commission, *Job Patterns for Minorities and Women in Private Industry, 1966*, Report No. 1 (Washington: The Commission, 1968), Part I, Table A1-4.

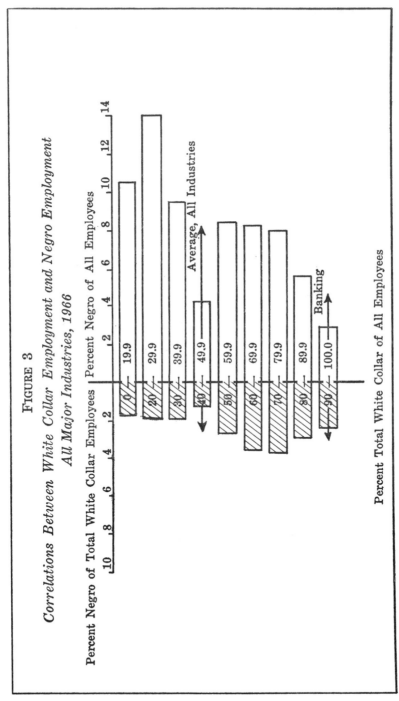

FIGURE 3

Correlations Between White Collar Employment and Negro Employment
All Major Industries, 1966

Source: U.S. Equal Employment Opportunity Commission, *Job Patterns for Minorities and Women in Private Industry, 1966*, Report No. 1 (Washington: The Commission, 1968), Part II.

Negro Preparation Levels

There are very few qualified Negro financiers seeking employment in the banking industry. Few members of that race have had any higher-level employment experience with banking and just as few have prepared themselves by garnering the necessary technological skills in college. Given the sociological condition of the country since the turn of the century, the severely restricted job horizons of Negroes until recently, and their general difficulty in acquiring either the experience or the training necessary for higher-level jobs in finance, this should not be unexpected. Even now, there are very few Negroes prepared for the highly specialized top jobs in banking where skill demands require developed sensitivities which are long in forming. But this argument begs the question, for the majority of white collar jobs in banking are not of this sort, being instead entry-level clerical positions, often machine oriented and highly routine. Some entry-level white collar bank jobs, far from requiring carefully developed skills and perceptions, demand little more than manual dexterity. Others, such as the teller positions, require arithmetical facility, an extensive array of good personal habits, and a reasonably sunny disposition as well. But in almost any of the clerical jobs, the minimum experience and skill required is of the high-school-level sort. As with the military so it is very largely true in banks that once the organization scheme has been devised, it can be manned by almost anyone. Therefore, the excuse commonly offered by bankers to the effect that the skills demanded by its white collar jobs are too rigorous for the current state of Negro preparedness is difficult to accept.

Entry-Level Expectations

Banks do prefer, and quite rightly, the best work force input possible for a given cost, and so prefer the experienced or at least the premotivated and adequately trained, not only to keep up standards, but also to protect themselves as much as possible against the dissatisfaction of employees of long standing.[19]

---

[19] *Wall Street Journal*, June 11, 1968: "Nation's Biggest Firms Now Committed to Help Solve the Racial Crisis." Quoting from the article: ". . . Corporate managers have to deal with another delicate problem—white backlash among workers who believe Negroes are getting preferential treatment or not doing their share of the work. 'We have to keep the bank running smoothly,' says Walter A. Hoadley, senior vice president and chief economist at the Bank of America. 'We have to prevent the people who aren't singled out (for special attention) from getting their noses out of joint.'"

A few years ago, when the job market was much looser, banks and other firms with high white collar demands could afford such selection procedures to seek entrants with more than minimal qualifications. In the tight labor markets of the 1960's, this sort of choosiness became a luxury. Almost all of the entry-level applicants seen by banks, white or black, come looking for positions equipped only with high-school-level sorts of minimal skill development. Banks throughout the country are increasingly forced to take up training programs for suitable development of those entry-level skills.

Most banks and other industries whose white collar positions are largely clerical have discovered that once such a training program has been set up, handling the incremental training which may be required by some of the Negroes is not particularly onerous. As a result, the Negro representation among new hires is rapidly increasing, especially in the larger, city banks. Between 1967 and 1968, Negroes were hired at a rate of more than 20 percent nationally, and about 27 percent in sixteen major cities. (See table 9 in chapter 3, and table 22 later in this chapter.) These figures indicate that the gap in Negro proportions between highly white collar industries, such as banking, and others is closing rapidly.

JOB REQUIREMENTS, PUBLIC CONTACT, AND PRODUCT DIFFERENTIATION

After "clerks," "tellers" compose the largest group under a single job title in the banking industry. (See tables 31 and 33 in chapter 6). The job is a demanding one in several respects, and the demands are intensified by the requirements of constant contact with the public. In Chapter II it was noted that certain skills are required, such as arithmetical ability and great care in handling cash. Additionally, there are many specific banking procedures with which a teller must be familiar. The American Bankers Association lists 117 such, which run the gamut from "wrapping coins" to "hold-up procedures," (but which do not, of course, include the instructions specific to individual banks).[20]

---

[20] The American Bankers Association, *How to Train A Bank Teller: A Management Guide*, A Training Pamphlet Prepared by the Committee on Employee Training and Country Bank Operations Committee (New York: The American Bankers Association, 1961), pp. 32-36.

But despite their complexities, learning these procedures and the technical content of the teller's job at least well enough to begin productive service should not take an overly long time for anyone who has demonstrated sufficient proficiency to get through high school. Indeed, the ABA-recommended training course requires but three weeks, and some simple "window" transactions are scheduled for the fourth day.

Customer Relations

The real problem with the teller job is not the job content, but the customer relations. In the words of the American Bankers Association:

> Most people who enter a bank do business principally with the tellers. As a result, tellers have a significant role in customer relations since they come directly in contact with customers more than any other employee in the bank. The success of a bank depends to a great extent on how well the tellers know and perform their jobs . . . An essential part of teller training is the developing of proper attitudes toward the public relations aspects of the job . . . If the customers' impressions, received through their contacts with tellers, are unfavorable, it is likely that they will take their business to another bank.[21]

It is for these reasons that banks are very concerned about the public presentability of those employed in this sensitive job, and the "traits and qualities the officer in charge of hiring should look for and evaluate during interviews," are the following (presented in the order listed by the American Bankers Association) : "Appearance, appropriate dress; poise, alertness, self-confidence; voice, mannerisms, ability to communicate; personality, friendliness, cooperative attitude; ambition; dependability; maturity; ability to get along well with people; interest in teller work and banking." [22]

The population which utilizes the services of banks is overwhelmingly white, and it is that population which is the final arbiter of the "appropriateness" of dress or the sufficiency of "friendliness" of a bank teller. For a long time, bankers throughout the country feared that any black would be debili-

---

[21] *Ibid.*, p. 9.

[22] *Ibid.*, p. 15.

tated by his lack of "appropriateness" in one or another of the factors above, and therefore unacceptable to a number of customers who would take their business elsewhere as a consequence of black hiring. Negro tellers were therefore employed by banks which had "Negro branches" and only rarely elsewhere.[23]

Product Differentiation

Another factor which intensifies the sensitivity of this job is the nondifferentiability of the product of the banking industry to the average customer. For handling the checking accounts, holding the time deposits, providing safe deposit facilities, and undertaking the other usual banking needs of customers, there is no essential difference between banks.[24] For most customers, therefore, there is no difficulty—outside of minor inconvenience—connected with changing banks, and the fear of customer reaction for a long time involved a genuine risk to the bank. Under these circumstances, one would expect to find fewer Negroes in public contact jobs generally (and in teller jobs specifically) than in other, less sensitive positions. This was the situation in banks until very recently.

Reaction to Employment of Negroes

In the survey of major banks conducted by the author in the Summer of 1968, one of the questions asked was: "What do you consider to be the greatest lack on the part of the Negro applicants for employment?" Some of the forty-nine bankers who responded gave multiple answers. The responses are ranked by frequency in Table 13.

About half of these responses have direct applicability to the public requirements of the teller job, and it is presumed that five years ago an even greater proportion of the answers would have tended to reflect veiled fears that Negro employees would be unacceptable to customers. Indeed, when asked, the bankers almost invariably admitted that they had harbored great fears

---

[23] For illustration of this point, see Bank F, table 28, in chapter 6.

[24] The author can attest to this personally, having utilized the services of seven different Philadelphia banks in a little over five years of residency. Two of the shifts were caused by dissatisfaction with attitudes of tellers or officers (all white, incidentally) but the balance were purely matters of locational convenience. There are no substantive differences in the type or variety of services offered or their costs.

—which they now agree were overdone—about customer reaction to an inflex of Negro jobholders. The actual reaction reported was very small, as witnessed in Table 14.

TABLE 13. *Bankers' Response to Question: "What Do You Consider the Greatest Lack On the Part of Negro Applicants for Employment?"*
47 Commercial Banks Surveyed
United States, 1968

Reply	Frequency of Reply
1. Basic education	18
2. Poor work history, skill development	12
3. Speech habits, verbal skills	9
4. Lack of empathy with whites, with profit system	7
5. Dress, personal hygiene	6
6. Lack of initiative, motivation	5
7. Lack of acceptable credentials	5
8. Lack of self-confidence	4
9. Super-sensitivity about race	1

Source: Data in the author's possession.

TABLE 14. *Reported Customer Reaction to Visible Negro Employees*
47 Commercial Banks Surveyed
United States, 1968

Type of Reaction	Severity		
	None	Minor	Severe
1. Letters of protest [a]	28	19	0
2. Letters of encouragement	29	17	1
3. Cancellation of deposits	43	4	0

Source: Data in the author's possession.

[a] Includes reaction to summer "hard-core" hiring projects.

Essentially, there were as many customers who either encouraged the banks to hire more Negroes (or congratulated them for having made a start in that direction) as there were customers who complained. Only four banks reported any cancellations of deposits which could be attributed to Negro hiring, and in no case could this manifestation of dissatisfaction be considered severe.

But the fears of reaction which had existed were real. As recently as 1964, in many cities in the South, only a very daring and adventurous personnel officer would have considered undertaking the risk of making his bank the only one in town to have Negro tellers. To break through this sort of situation, concerted action is required—either voluntary or legislated. So long as one personnel man alone had to run the risk of a possible bigoted reaction by customers, there was little reason for him to contemplate hiring Negro tellers, regardless of his personel feelings on the subject. However, if all of the major banks in the city agreed to take on Negro tellers (or were required to) then there could be no major problem, for the only alternative possible to a dissatisfied customer would be to keep his money under his mattress, and this is an alternative which only the hardiest of bigots rich enough to matter would contemplate.

Thus, for banks which had not yet hired Negro tellers, the Civil Rights Act of 1964 and Executive Order 11246 provided not only the necessity but also the excuse to break the racial barriers surrounding public contact jobs. The subsequent hiring of tellers by banks and the lack of difficulties attendant to it invalidated the "fear of reaction" argument and also prevented its use as a "pass the buck" excuse for nonaction—as it may have been used by some bankers.[25]

---

[25] The author made a very informal survey of his current branch bank which does a brisk, if somewhat seasonal, business. On average, three of the tellers in the bank are Negro, three white. The customers are predominantly white, but on the crowded days there are usually some Negro customers as well. Over seven visits, no pattern of any sort was discernible in the racial use of tellers. That is, customers of both races used tellers of both races on a basis which was apparently purely random. The only other pattern which was clear concerned one "favorite" teller, a Negro girl, whose pleasant disposition and efficiency invariably earned her the longest lines of customers.

REQUIREMENT FOR PROFITS

To see how strong a factor the requirement for profits is in affecting Negro employment, we shall compare the experience of commercial banks with those of the Federal Reserve Banks. There are twelve Federal Reserve Banks in the country, one for each of the Federal Reserve Districts. Each of these banks, except for Philadelphia and Boston, has from one to four branches, located for geographical convenience. There are a total of twenty-four such branches. The Federal Reserves are "bankers' banks," and do no business with the general public. Each is a corporation organized and operated for public service, and as such is not a profit-seeking institution. The directors of each of the banks are general businessmen rather than bankers, and not "officers, directors, employees, or stockholders of any bank." [26]

Although major financial policies are closely controlled by the Board of Governors in Washington, this is not so much the case for personnel policies.[27] The banks in no way enjoy a "protected" status and their employees are not on the civil service rolls. The banks are made more conscious of new federal employment policy requirements by their Board of Governors and seem faster to respond to new requirements and directives. But they, too, have had their reviews by human relations commissions, visits from CORE, union organization attempts, and other varieties of external pressures. They are disbursed all over the country; their size in 1966 (including branches), ran from just over fifty employees to almost 3,700; their wages were about the same as those paid by commercial banks: "Our raw wages are some-

---

[26] Board of Governors of the Federal System, *The Federal Reserve System; Purposes and Functions* (Washington, 1961), p. 70.

[27] According to Andrew Brimmer, member of the Federal Reserve Board of Governors, Negro employment in the Federal Reserve Banks is "supported by a strong positive employment policy developed by the Federal Reserve Board;" but Dr. Brimmer goes on to point out: "Despite a strong endorsement by policy officials in the System, the performance is uneven among Reserve Banks." [In: Andrew F. Brimmer, *Employment Patterns and the Quest for Equal Opportunity in Banking*, A Report Before a Conference on Bank Employment Practices Sponsored by U.S. Treasury Department and the Michigan Human Relations Commission, Lansing, Michigan, May 22, 1968 (Washington: Board of Governors of the Federal Reserve System, 1968), pp. 14, 15.] This suggests that, rather than detailed policy directives, the individual Reserve Banks are given suggestions for policy direction and provided somewhat closer review than are commercial banks, but are not subject to employment policy control as such.

what lower, but with fringes may even be a bit on the high side." [28]

In the light of all this, it would be expected that the Federal Reserve Banks might have *slightly* greater Negro employment than commercial banks. In fact, their Negro employment is considerably higher, as seen in Table 15. The table shows that Federal Reserve Banks had more than twice the Negro employment rate of commercial banks. In addition to their having no tellers or other public-contact employees, there are some other job classification differences which become apparent from a study of the table. The Federal Reserve Banks have relatively more blue collar jobs (or at least classified more jobs as such) and these jobs were both more heavily male and more heavily Negro than blue collar positions in commercial banks. On the other hand, white collar jobs in the Federal Reserve Banks were held by a greater predominance of females. Of all the white collar jobs held by Negroes, three out of four were filled by females. The average number of employees in 1966 at the Federal Reserve Banks (545) is fairly close to the average number of employees in a field sample of 738 commercial banks (510). But the Federal Reserves averaged forty-nine Negroes per bank as compared to twenty-two.

The difference cannot be explained by absolute size, relative size, geographical location, government requirements, or wages offered. Job differences and job classification differences, lack of public-contact requirements, closer association with federal policy, and lack of requirements for profits have apparently had effect on managements' policy determinations.

Comparisons with Other Financial Institutions

Other financial institutions which perform services somewhat related to those of commercial banks but do not have the two unique characteristics of the Federal Reserve Banks—closer association with federal policies, and lack of profit requirements—show about the same Negro work force proportions as do commercial banks. Institutions of this sort are: mutual savings banks, trust companies not engaged in deposit banking, currency exchanges and safe deposit companies, and a variety of credit agencies—including savings and loan associations. These institutions have jobs and job classifications similar to those of banks,

---

[28] Interview, June 1968.

TABLE 15. *Federal Reserve Banks and All Commercial Banks Employment by Race and Sex United States, 1966*

Type of Bank	All Commercial Banks	Federal Reserve Banks
Number of Banks Reporting	738	35
All Employees	376,017	19,080
White collar	352,428	15,786
Ma.e white collar	144,905	5,819
Female white collar	207,523	9,967
White collar as percent of all employees	93.7	82.7
All Negro Employees	16,561	1,727
Negro white collar	11,011	891
Male white collar	3,403	201
Female white collar	7,608	690
Negro white collar as percent of all Negro employees	66.5	51.6
Negroes as percent of all employees	4.4	9.1
Negro white collar as percent of total white collar	3.1	5.6
Total females as percent of all employees	57.0	55.8
Female white collar as percent of total white collar	58.9	63.1
Negro female white collar as percent of total Negro white collar	69.1	77.4

Source: Table 9 and data in author's possession.

although many of them are free from extensive public contact requirements. All of them do require profits. A 1966 field survey of employment patterns in 58 mutual savings banks found that this group had the highest Negro representation in the banking and finance industry, with 5.4 percent Negro overall, and 4.6 percent in white collar jobs.

Companies not engaged in deposit banking, currency exchanges, and safe deposit companies similarly show Negro employment levels slightly higher than those in commercial banks. Credit agencies, security dealers and exchanges, and insurance and other miscellaneous financial services have somewhat smaller Negro employment ratios than do the commercial banks.[29]

THE REQUIREMENTS OF TRUSTWORTHINESS

The close proximity of a great deal of cash, especially when it is changing hands rapidly, provides a very real and understandable temptation for those who would like to find for it a better home than they feel its rightful owner could provide. The degree of temptation varies with the amount of cash and with the looseness of control. In department stores, where tight control is very difficult to maintain, it has been found that many of the losses which had been attributed to shop-lifting customers were actually attributable to employees. Banks have very tight controls, but the amounts handled are much larger than in department stores, and the temptations consequently greater. As a result, banks are very sensitive about the trustworthiness of employees, and seek to do whatever possible to insure themselves against internal thievery and deceit.

Employment Investigations

All of the major banks in the country are members of the Federal Deposit Insurance Corporation, membership in which requires bonding of all guards, tellers, and others who handle money. The FDIC provides relatively stiff penalties for any bank which knowingly employs persons with past criminal convictions of either a major type or involving breach of trust or other crimes against property. For this reason, as well as several others, banks have traditionally been very careful about checking the records of applicants. Checking with the local

---

[29] U.S. Equal Employment Opportunities Commission, *op. cit.*, Part II.

police, running fingerprints through the FBI files, and performing very careful checks of personal and past employment references are quite common. Some banks go further, requiring polygraph tests of applicants for particularly sensitive jobs such as teller or guard. (Only one of forty-seven sample banks in the author's survey follows this practice, and apparently that organization is somewhat sensitive about it, as no information concerning polygraphs was volunteered to the author.) [30]

The primary purpose of these investigations is to identify and restrict from the temptations those who either have demonstrated an untoward desire for large sums of other peoples' money, or whose history is such as to indicate a proclivity in that direction. It is for this reason that banks rely heavily on credit bureau checks to find the stability of the applicants' personal financial situation. Banks also increasingly require physical examinations, where evidences of narcotics addiction can be discovered.

Of the forty-seven banks visited during the author's survey, nine reported that they did no deliberate checking outside of a few spot reference checks, ten checked references extensively, twelve used the services of the FBI, fifteen made at least spot checks with the local police, and twenty-seven made credit checks. (At least six reported requiring physicals, but not all banks were asked about this, and tallies were not kept.)

Effect on Negro Employment

In the large metropolitan areas, where most of the bank hiring that we are dealing with here takes place, the overall crime rate is twice what it is in smaller cities and three times that of rural areas. Dope addiction is almost exclusively a city problem. For whatever sociological reasons, Negroes make up a larger than proportional share of both criminals and addicts, and this affects their employability in some cases. For example, several banks had to seek special dispensation from FDIC in reference to past arrests on the part of "hard-core" youths for summer

---

[30] In states where the practice is legal, many banks do employ polygraph testing as an investigative device in the event of "mysterious disappearance" of funds. The problem here is that the device is nonselective, and the investigators are liable to uncover misdeeds in which they have no particular interest and which, having been discovered, pose serious difficulties to the investigators in determining what should be done with the information. A polygraph investigation into a theft in one bank, for example, turned up the information that two of the tellers (who had had nothing to do with the theft) were homosexual.

employment under the National Alliance of Businessmen program.

But much more important than involvement with crime or past convictions so far as Negro employment is concerned, are difficulties arising from mishandling of personal finances and the risks attendant to this. Undoubtedly this problem will attenuate as the Negro population becomes increasingly middle-class in its outlooks and aspirations, but for the time being the existence of large numbers of jobs in the banking industry for which bad financial or legal history involves considerable risk to the employer makes that industry somewhat less receptive to Negro applicants than would be the case in most industries.

HIGH SCHOOL OUTPUT MATCH

In New York City, where about 40 percent of all high school students who will be gradulated this year are minority group members, the females far outnumber the males. This is also true in other cities throughout the country. Both the female and the Negro proportions of high school graduating classes are increasing, and additionally, more and more of the graduating girls are seeking employment. Those industries which have a high demand for this level of labor input, and such is the case with banks, should show higher levels of Negro female employment than industries which do not have this characteristic. This does not appear to be the case in the banking industry, and we can only assume that the level of Negro female employment would be even lower were so many Negro girls not graduating and entering the labor market.

INDUSTRY IMAGE AND HISTORICAL PATTERNS

If an industry is thought of as a good place to work by any particular segment of the job market, then the members of that segment will be likely to seek employment there, regardless of what the job demands and characteristics actually are. College students, for example, often seek sales jobs during the summer vacation months even though they could generally get more free time, better pay, and far better experience with a blue collar job or other industrial position. An even better example of the pull of "image" is provided by the appeal to young girls of the stewardess job with airlines. Conversely, an industry whose image is such as to be unattractive to some segment of the job market will have much more difficulty appealing to that segment. An image, once established, is very difficult to change.

Banking Image

The stereotype image of the banking industry portrays that industry as conservative, changeless, dull, low-paying, with few opportunities for rapid advancement. The teller line, which sets the image for the clerical-level jobs, currently retains more prestige in the eyes of banks than in the eyes of the potential applicants who often understand the job to be underpaid and requiring extensive technical skills and enforced precision.

There are some other characteristics of the job which serve to frighten applicants. It is apparent from the physical construction of teller windows that little freedom of action for social intercourse is possible on the job between employees, but the constant contact required with bank-using public must be both courteous and extremely careful. It is not a position in which the job holder can enhance his self-image by exerting influence over those with whom he must deal. It is not a job on which a person can ever relax. It has none of the aspects of being a "fun job" and seems more unforgiving than most.

Higher-level jobs in banking often present the same limited appeal to college graduates, MBA's, and others who compare industries in search of a first managerial position. The image of low pay, long training periods, slow advancement, and lack of excitement serves to limit the appeal of the industry.

In sum, banking is not an industry which has been treated well in the public press or by public sentiment. All told, with the possible exception of the popular view of "bankers' hours," there is little inherent in the image of the industry to attract those who are not premotivated to be well disposed toward it; and on managerial as well as clerical entrant levels, there is little reason for Negroes to be premotivated toward the industry.

Negro Experience and Preidentification with Banking

In Appendix B, where the history and status of all-Negro banks are presented, several aspects of banking prior to World War II which served to make Negroes very distrustful of the industry are discussed. The Freedmen's Bank, which was supposed to be a bank run specifically for Negroes and which appeared to many to have the protection of the federal government, failed in the panic of 1873, and in failing destroyed not only the savings but also the faith of many of its depositors in any banking system. Among the all-Negro banks which followed the Freedmen's Bank, a rather high proportion failed in their infancies; this further shook the confidence of Negroes in banking. For many years, the regular commercial banks would not handle the accounts of Negroes, much less accept Negro participation as employees actively associated with the industry.

All of these, and other factors, combine into a general disassociation of Negroes from the industry and, as was also the case with many rural Americans generally, (although from different reasons), Negroes took to storing any excess funds in the cookie jar, or subsequently, in the Postal Savings System. Sociologically, there were many evil connotations connected with the industry, which the upheavals caused by periodic bank panics did little to dispell. Negroes were, and still are, among the hardest hit by depressions, and many were of the opinion that depressions were *caused* by bankers and other financiers.

More so for that race than for other ethnic groups, Negroes have had very little experience with banks as either users or employees. Thus, with some justification, they dislike banks more than most other industries and more than most other ethnic groups do. Therefore there has been little reason for Negroes to aspire to or prepare themselves for employment in that industry as they might for other professions.

Because of these factors, Negroes on all levels lack premotivation towards the industry. Even now, if banks are to be able to recruit many Negro employees having high levels of potential for development, they must be able to make the industry seem attractive to them and present an enticing image. The alternative for banks is to be content with less than the best, watching other industries absorb the most talented Negroes while banks themselves have to undertake extensive training programs.

PRESTIGE AND WAGE LEVELS

As we have mentioned, there usually is considerable difference between the image which an industry has in the eyes of its job seekers and the actuality of the job itself. If the image is positive, industries can often capitalize on it. Going back to a previous example, the airlines are very happy with, and protective of, the excitement and apparent desirability of the stewardess' jobs for the obvious reason that if the image is accepted, then the lines can, to at least some degree, pay their stewardesses with "excitement" rather than with cash. If the job were alternatively conceived of as the hectic, unrewarding, morally and physically dangerous, dead end, flying waitress job it sometimes is, the cash inducements which would have to be offered by the lines to get applicants would have to be considerably higher even than they are now.

Some years ago, despite the sociological and mental demands which we have outlined for the teller's job in banks, the position was considered to have prestige, and as a result banks remunerated tellers (and other employees, by association) partially in this quantity and partially in dollars. But the prestige attached to the job and to working in banking instead of in a manufacturing firm has attenuated. What has happened to banking wages?

Wage Levels

Bankers often seem horrified by the situation, but they are fond of pointing out that clerical wages have been going up rapidly in the last few years, and that managerial entrants are being offered "salaries which would have been unheard of five years ago." [31] It is quite true that bank wages and salaries have been on the upswing; in the last ten years, the average weekly wage of nonsupervisory employees in banking has increased by 50 percent. Highly-placed bank personnel men throughout the country seem overwhelmingly of the opinion that past wage differentials between their industry and others have already been or are rapidly being closed. Of the forty-seven who were asked by the author, two claimed their wages to be higher than manufacturing; four said wages were on par with local nonmanufacturing firms; five felt their wages were at least higher than other banks'; and two professed to have the highest banking wages in the country. Five felt they could not compete with government wage scales (not all were asked); four reported unmeetable competition from some specific local industry; and only four stated their clerical wages were lower than those of-

---

[31] Interview with a southern bank personnel director, August 1968.

fered by other major employers in the area. Twenty-six firms indicated parity in clerical wages with area industry.[32]

Unfortunately, although the consensus here is one of wages trending toward parity, this does not seem to be the case in actuality. Figures released by the U.S. Department of Labor Statistics covering average median wages for 1966-1967 in finance (including savings and loans, insurance, and real estate) and manufacturing show financial wages to suffer by the comparison.[33] These are shown in Table 16.[34] Notice there that although finance employees on average fare better with respect to the male janitors employed (generally taken as the lowest-level job and used as the base standard in the table) than do manufacturing employees in the same jobs with respect to their janitors, this distinction is rather hollow when it is seen that the wages of male janitors in manufacturing are about 20 percent higher than those of their finance counterparts. The final result is that clerical employees in finance in thirty-five of the thirty-six job categories noted make less per hour.

Checking comparative figures in various issues of the *Monthly Labor Review* reveals additionally that the banking industry is the lowest paying segment of the financial group. By those figures, through October 1968, only workers in the garment trades and retail sales, hotel workers, laundry workers, canners, and cigar rollers average to a smaller hourly wage than nonsupervisory bank workers do.

Figure 4 is a composite figure arrived at by using data from several different statistical series. Nevertheless, the indications are pretty clear that banking wages, although they have risen appreciably since 1948, are barely maintaining a proportional lag behind total private industry wages.

---

[32] There are several overlapping categories here, so the frequencies reported in each category do not total to forty-seven. Several bankers said they either would not or could not answer the question.

[33] Donald J. Blackmore, "Occupational Wage Relationships in Metropolitan Areas," *Monthly Labor Review*, Vol. XCI (December 1968).

[34] The table as presented is in a modified format. The Bureau of Labor Statistics showed only wage relatives to average janitorial wages. As these janitorial wages were also presented in the same article, we have simply multiplied them out to arrive at the hourly wage rates.

TABLE 16. *Average Hourly Earnings*
Financial and Manufacturing Establishments in Metropolitan
Areas, 1966-1967

	Median Establishment			
Office - Clerical Occupational Group	Average hourly earnings as percent of average for men janitors		Average hourly earnings	
	Finance	Manufacturing	Finance	Manufacturing
Men				
Clerks, accounting, class A	152	128	3.01	3.03
Clerks, accounting, class B	124	106	2.46	2.51
Clerks, payroll	128	126	2.53	2.99
Office boys	95	82	1.88	1.94
Tabulating-machine operators, class A	148	133	2.93	3.15
Tabulating-machine operators, class B	130	116	2.57	2.75
Tabulating-machine operators, class C	111	100	2.20	2.37
Women				
Bookkeeping-machine operators, class A	121	114	2.40	2.70
Bookkeeping-machine operators, class B	108	103	2.14	2.44
Clerks, accounting, class A	134	122	2.65	2.89
Clerks, accounting, class B	108	98	2.14	2.32
Clerks, file, class A	117	99	2.32	2.35
Clerks, file, class B	95	88	1.88	2.09
Clerks, file, class C	88	84	1.74	1.99
Clerks, payroll	131	110	2.59	2.61
Comptometer operators	101	98	2.00	2.32
Duplicating-machine operators	107	90	2.12	2.13
Keypunch operators, class A	116	104	2.30	2.46
Keypunch operators, class B	104	93	2.06	2.20
Office girls	84	78	1.66	1.85
Secretaries	145	122	2.87	2.89
Stenographers, general	108	98	2.14	2.32
Stenographers, senior	123	108	2.44	2.56
Switchboard operators, class A	121	104	2.40	2.46
Switchboard operators, class B	113	101	2.24	2.39
Switchboard operators-receptionists	116	100	2.30	2.37
Tabulating-machine operators, class A	143	127	2.83	3.01
Tabulating-machine operators, class B	132	114	2.61	2.70
Tabulating-machine operators, class C	105	102	2.08	2.42
Transcribing-machine operators, general	98	97	1.94	2.30
Typists, class A	109	98	2.16	2.32
Typists, class B	95	88	1.88	2.09

Source: Donald J. Blackmore, "Occupational Wage Relationships in Metropolitan Areas," *Monthly Labor Review*, Vol. XCI (December 1968), pp. 30-31.

Note: Average male janitor wages: manufacturing, $2.37; finance, $1.98.

COMBINED EFFECT OF IMAGE AND WAGES

The low pull of the wage levels combined with the lack of other Negro predisposition toward seeking entrance to clerical-level jobs has effects in three areas—the first concerning the quality level of job seekers generally, the second concerning the quality level of Negro applicants, and the third concerning the importance of communications from the banks to potential job seekers.

The attenuation of the prestige image of the most visible banking job (and the lack of a product to identify with) means that more and more applicants come to the bank for employment simply as an alternative to looking for a job at the gas company or at the widget works, and many either will accept the higher wages of those alternatives, or will join the bank as a temporary measure until one of the higher-paying jobs becomes available. Some also join to get the experience necessary to be able to apply for a job with government. The results generally are being felt by the banks in the form of less qualified applicants, higher training costs, and greater turnover.

We have seen that both image and wages have combined to produce even less preidentification by Negroes, so all of these effects are magnified when it comes to them. The results are that banks see fewer employable Negroes than they could, and therefore employ fewer than other industries which do not have these problems. In both cases (and for entrance jobs on managerial levels as well) the burdens on bank communications for recruiting are intensified, and recruiters have to do a better "selling job" on their industry than do recruiters from other firms.

DISCRIMINATION

It is clearly the consensus of Americans, black and white, that the tradition of racial discrimination against Negroes no longer reflects current value orderings of the society and should be scrapped. But tradition is a strong thing, and there is little point to wishing for a different history by recasting the mores of our past society and re-interpreting its actions in terms of our current value structure.

The racial discrimination which was practiced in this country against Negroes a few years ago was in keeping with the then current ideas of acceptable behavior on the part of the majority.

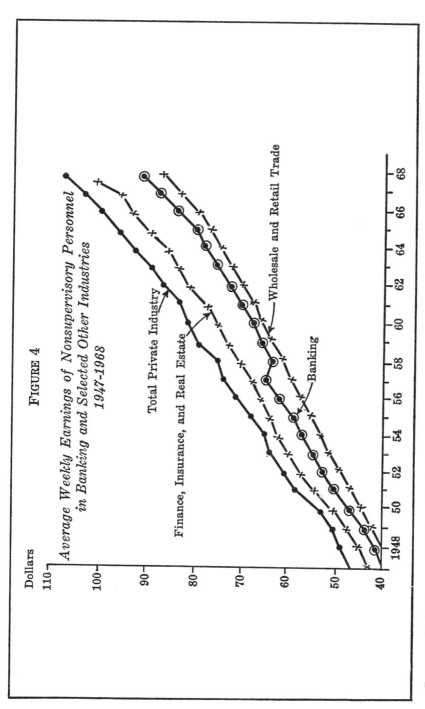

FIGURE 4

Average Weekly Earnings of Nonsupervisory Personnel in Banking and Selected Other Industries 1947-1968

Total Private Industry

Finance, Insurance, and Real Estate

Wholesale and Retail Trade

Banking

Source: U.S. Bureau of Labor Statistics, *Employment and Earnings and Monthly Report on the Labor Force,* Vol. 15, April 1969.

Let us be thankful that ideas of acceptable behavior have changed, and that most persons have agreed that the change constitutes an advancement of the civilization. Let us also admit that some have not made the transition.

There are those who will point out that our current society is so positive about its existing value structure that it has solidified into law proscriptions of discrimination, making illegal the traditions which had supported it. And this is true. However, discrimination, much more so than, say, embezzlement, is a state of mind resulting in an entire behavioral pattern, only parts of which can be given the attention of the law. And anything not specifically covered by the law must be left to tradition.

The sad fact is that even were verifiable discrimination (e.g., refusal to interview Negroes for employment, refusal to serve Negroes in the usual way for the usual fees) completely absent from the society—and it is not—the disguisable sort of bigotry consisting of isolation, nastiness, and various other forms of following the letter but not the spirit of the law will persist and can have the same exclusionary effect. It takes much longer to build the mutual trust and understanding between the races which is required for this form of discrimination to attenuate; and while it is definitely attenuating, it does persist. The question we are facing here is: Is there anything about any particular industry, specifically banking, which would lead one to believe that its officials are *more* bigoted or *more* likely to practice discrimination against Negroes than officials of other industries?

We know that it took longer for bankers to break the all-white tradition of their industry than was required by various others, and we know that the proportion of employment which is Negro is less than the average in most other industries. But if we are to believe that this slowness and relative lack of response is attributable to a higher degree of residue discrimination among bankers, we must be able to demonstrate that something about officials' jobs in banking tends to attract a higher proportion of bigots to that occupation than are attraced to manufacturing. We know, of course, that some bankers discriminate, just as we know some manufacturers discriminate. But we do not know if, or why, more bankers than manufacturers do.

The only sociological factors of which we are aware having general application are two: whites in the lower economic and social classes tend to be more susceptible to practicing discrimination; and among southerners of all classes the tradition that way is stronger. But southerners do not dominate the banking industry and no one would contend that officials of the industry are drawn from the lowest economic orders. There is a somewhat more specialized argument mounted by the EEOC to the effect that although all employers are bigoted, the discrimination becomes more virulent as the jobs involved become more prestigeous; that although some whites are now willing to help Negroes onto the economic ladder, they are willing to help them only onto the bottom rung. The evidence cited for this is in two forms. First, white collar industries employ a smaller proportion of Negroes than blue collar industries; and second, there are extremely few Negroes on top of organizations, and few Negroes in any of the jobs considered especially prestigeous on any level (as secretary to an executive would be on the clerical levels).

We have indicated before, in discussing Figure 3 in this chapter, that we do not find the first of these arguments to be particularly compelling. However, it is undoubtedly true that many corporate leaders, in the interest of prudence, will require a more positive demonstration of potential from Negroes before their promotion to economically sensitive or policy formulating positions than they will from whites with whose aspirations, reactions, and behavior patterns they are more familiar. And since there are relatively more such positions in banking than in manufacturing, the effect of this caution will be more visible. On the other hand, higher-level positions and prestigeous jobs on any level are normally positions of reward for past performance, potential, and a variety of other factors, and are seldom chosen by lot. Experimentation cannot be extreme for jobs which are honestly sensitive. For any of these jobs, it is difficult to say where prudence leaves off and discrimination begins. We therefore can find scant evidence which would support the contention that more bigotry exists in the banking industry than in other corporations, and suggest that insofar as banking employs fewer Negroes the reasons for that must be found in more specific arguments. We do not exclude the possibility that in many of the specific arguments bankers' decision making is influenced by lack of experience with, or lack of understanding of, Negro value structures, motivations, reactions, and general behavior patterns.

CONCLUSIONS

With the exception of the demand by banks for large numbers of high school girls, all of the other factors which we have identified as serving to differentiate the banking industry from manufacturing concerns—including its job requirements, image, and wage levels—also serve to make the climate of the industry less hospitable to Negroes. We have also seen that recent developments in the evolution of the industry are tending to obviate these differences. We expect that banking statistics will much more closely approximate the national averages for Negro employment in the near future. Although the banking industry was one of the last to begin hiring Negroes in any numbers, overt bigotry does not appear to have been the exclusive or even a major cause—except insofar as racial discrimination was a standard behavior pattern of all employers prior to about 1960.

On the basis of the analyses here, and on the basis of the attitudes found among banking personnel managers, some of which were summarized in Chapter III, it is our prediction that the Negro representation in banking will continue to increase at a minimum of 15 and perhaps as high as 22 or 23 percent per annum compounded, continuing the trend which began in about 1960. Unless there is some sharp change in attitude one way or the other toward Negro employment, we shall expect the banking industry Negro employment proportion to approximate the nation's Negro population proportion by about 1972, as shown in Figure 2 in Chapter III.

During this same time period, we shall expect to see somewhat higher Negro representation in the officers and managers job classification, but do not expect that the Negro proportion in those jobs will be as high as for clerical employment.

CHAPTER V.

Variation in Negro Employment
Within the Banking Industry

Among the forty-six commercial banks which supplied statistical data to the author, Negro employment ranged from a 1968 low of 1.0 percent to 21.2 percent of the work force when the data are arranged by city, the Seattle banks' average of 1.4 percent Negro was low, and the figures ranged up to the sixteen city high of 19.2 percent in the District of Columbia. When the reports from all banks from that year are arranged by states and averaged (excluding the District of Columbia, Hawaii, and Alaska), the employment proportion runs from a low of 0.0 percent in New Hampshire, North Dakota, South Dakota, and Vermont to a high of 10.0 percent in New York. Obviously, the variation around the industry's 5.9 percent average 1968 Negro employment is very great.

The last chapter discussed various aspects of the banking industry which served to differentiate it from other industries and which seemed to affect the relative level of Negro employment. Here we turn our attenion to analysis of factors important to the industry which seem to be responsible for the internal variation in Negro employment within the industry.

To make this analysis, we shall look in turn at historical hiring patterns in various areas of the country and at the availability of Negro applicants; at the affect of organizational flexibility arising from large size and from decentralization; and at the effect of the presence of other minority groups. There are some other differences internal to the industry which will obviously produce variations in Negro employment levels, such as the perceptions of individual personnel officers and the policies of individual banking establishments. These will be taken up in a later chapter.

REGIONAL HIRING PATTERNS

Any discussion of hiring patterns in banking or in any other industry requires attention to the historical patterns of the South. It would be less than realistic to suppose that the traditions of

TABLE 17.   *The Banking Industry*
Employment by Race, Region, and State, 1966

Region and State	All Employees	Negro	Percent Negro
South Region			
Alabama	4,943	226	4.6
Arkansas	1,645	87	5.3
Delaware	2,361	74	3.1
D.C.	4,103	493	12.0
Florida	8,211	280	3.4
Georgia	7,659	462	6.0
*Kentucky	1,884	82	4.4
Louisiana	5,595	463	8.3
Maryland	8,482	454	5.4
*Mississippi	—	—	—
North Carolina	10,699	639	6.0
Oklahoma	2,700	73	2.7
South Carolina	3,113	164	5.3
Tennessee	6,926	505	7.3
Texas	17,202	973	5.7
Virginia	9,520	702	7.4
*West Virginia	407	20	4.9
Total	95,450	5,697	6.0

Percent of total banking employment   18.9
Percent of total Negro employment   25.4

Region and State	All Employees	Negro	Percent Negro
Northeast Region			
Connecticut	9,163	257	2.8
*Maine	1,936	1	0.1
Massachusetts	18,895	492	2.6
*New Hampshire	115	—	—
New Jersey	16,765	604	3.6
New York	114,338	6,401	5.6
Pennsylvania	33,115	1,065	3.2
*Rhode Island	3,410	53	1.6
*Vermont	743	—	—
Total	198,480	8,873	4.5

Percent of total banking employment   39.3
Percent of total Negro employment   39.6

TABLE 17. (Continued)

Region and State	All Employees	Negro	Percent Negro
North Central Region			
Illinois	24,209	1,252	5.2
Indiana	8,570	299	3.5
*Iowa	1,769	26	1.5
*Kansas	1,103	30	2.7
Michigan	21,095	1,070	5.1
Minnesota	5,581	83	1.5
Missouri	9,514	678	7.1
*Nebraska	1,893	40	2.1
*North Dakota	—	—	—
Ohio	17,752	881	5.0
*South Dakota	141	1	0.7
Wisconsin	4,672	52	1.1
Total	96,299	4,412	4.6
Percent of total banking employment	19.1		
Percent of total Negro employment	19.7		
West Region			
Arizona	5,998	94	1.6
California	80,075	3,081	3.8
Colorado	3,213	83	2.6
*Idaho	2,267	1	**
*Montana	689	2	0.3
Nevada	1,942	23	1.2
*New Mexico	931	—	—
Oregon	7,844	50	0.6
Utah	2,306	—	—
Washington	9,824	71	0.7
*Wyoming	—	—	—
Total	115,089	3,405	3.0
Percent of total banking employment	22.8		
Percent of total Negro employment	15.2		

Source: U. S. Equal Employment Opportunity Commission, *Job Patterns for Minorities and Women in Private Industry, 1966*, Report No. 1 (Washington: The Commission, 1968), Part II, Data for states marked (*) were estimated from a field sample of 738 banks in the author's possession.

Note: Because of the variety of sources used, totals are not identical with those reported in other tables reported in Chapter III.

** Less than 0.05 percent.

the South concerning Negroes have not had an effect on employment levels there, and normally it would be safe to assume that in banking as in other industries, the progress of the southern Negroes toward employment equality would have been much retarded.[35] Especially because of banking's lack of menial, laborer, and "muscle-power" jobs (and because of most of the other factors mentioned in the last chapter), we would expect the southern employer attiudes to be visible in the statistics.

As a first approximation to understanding the regional differences, the data in Table 17 have been compiled from the overall, 1966 employment statistics. The regional breakdowns used are those of the Bureau of the Census.

Discrimination and the South

Looking at the Negro participation on the table for banks in the individual states provides the first notice that the automatic and offhand dismissal of the South as the ultimate locus of racial discrimination in banking may bear some re-examination. Among the sixteen states which are comprised by the southern region of the country, twelve showed Negro participation at a rate higher than the national average. This compared with only one out of nine for the Northeast, four out of eleven for the North Central region, and none out of ten for the West. (No data were available from three states: Mississippi, North Dakota, and Wyoming.) For the South as a whole, Negro participation was at twice the rate of the West. (The conclusions are not greatly affected by taking the smaller area breakdowns also used by the Bureau of the Census.) The figures in Table 17 also show that for all of the Negroes employed in banking, more than 25 percent were employed in the South, although less than 19 percent of the total banking population was in that region. The situation for the West is almost exactly reversed.

There are some other interesting data which give rise to similar results, and these are the data derived from the tabulation of the number of reporting units in the banking industry which showed no Negro employment at all. The data, taken from a field sample of 738 banks in 1966, are presented as Figure 5, where it is shown that whereas fourteen reporting units from the South, with a total of 1,700 employees, had no Negro employ-

---

[35] Some southerners honestly disagree, arguing that there is no more discrimination in the South than in any other area with equivalent Negro population. We shall develop this point subsequently in the chapter.

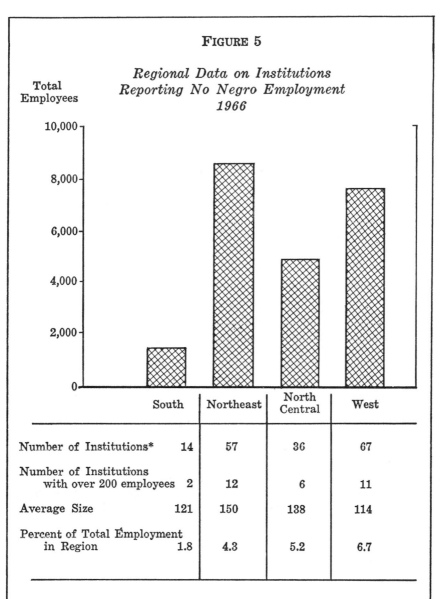

FIGURE 5

Regional Data on Institutions
Reporting No Negro Employment
1966

	South	Northeast	North Central	West
Number of Institutions*	14	57	36	67
Number of Institutions with over 200 employees	2	12	6	11
Average Size	121	150	138	114
Percent of Total Employment in Region	1.8	4.3	5.2	6.7

* Separate reporting units; some may be branches.

Source: Data in author's possession

ment, sixty-seven reporting units from the West had a total of 7,662 employees with no Negroes among them. In total, 1.8 percent of all employees working in the South worked in banks in which they had no Negro co-workers. This compares with 6.7 percent in the West, 5.2 percent in the North Central region, and 4.3 percent in the Northeast.

Growth in Negro Employment

Additional insight into regional patterns can be gained by examining the regional and state totals and breakdowns for 1967 and 1968. These, together with the Negro share in the growth of the industry between the years are shown in Table 18.

The table shows a relative change, both since the 1966 figures of Table 17 and also internally, between 1967 and 1968. Banking in the South region of the country seems to be growing somewhat faster than elsewhere, and in 1968 it represents a greater proportion of the total industry work force; but the Negro representation, while increasing from a high base (relative to the other regions) is not growing at as fast a rate as elsewhere. The "Negro share of growth" column in the table is most indicative of this. Notice that between 1967 and 1968, 12.5 percent of all banking employment growth was Negro in the South, but this is compared with a high of 30.0 percent in the Northeast. (Incidentally, although the South trails the rest of the country in this, 12.5 percent is still slightly higher than the country's Negro population proportion, and it is pleasant to note that were even the lowest rate perpetuated throughout the country gross *statistical* discrimination would eventually become a thing of the past.) Certainly, the case is much stronger in the Northeast which, dominated by New York, shows very great gains for this year. Those gains were sufficient that since 1966, the Northeast region has overtaken the South as the relative leader in Negro employment.

Before moving on, it should be noted that firms representing the industry in four Western states shrank in employment during a period of general banking expansion and it is interesting to see that in all four—Montana, Nevada, New Mexico, and Washington—the Negro proportion of the remaining employment was greater than before. Although these banks had few Negroes to begin with, the Negroes were, by and large, the "last hired"; apparently, they were not the "first fired." We hasten to add that there is no indication that such might be the case in a large-scale

TABLE 18. *The Banking Industry*
Employment by Race, Region, and State
1967-1968

Region and State	1967			1968			Percent Negro Share of Growth[a]
	All Employees	Negro	Percent Negro	All Employees	Negro	Percent Negro	
South Region							
Alabama	4,795	147	3.1	4,962	202	4.1	32.9
Arkansas	1,836	91	5.0	1,919	102	5.3	13.3
Delaware	1,997	73	3.7	2,251	114	5.1	16.1
D.C.[b]	4,282	691	16.1	5,181	958	18.5	29.7
Florida	12,158	401	3.3	12,686	504	4.0	19.5
Georgia	8,431	561	6.7	9,054	663	7.3	16.4
Kentucky	3,653	206	5.6	4,041	261	6.5	14.2
Louisiana	5,838	506	8.7	5,926	406	6.9	*
Maryland	6,806	365	5.4	7,261	419	5.8	11.9
Mississippi	2,615	111	4.2	2,839	134	4.7	10.3
North Carolina	10,565	704	6.7	11,572	751	6.5	4.7
Oklahoma	3,586	93	2.6	3,625	121	3.3	71.8
South Carolina	2,077	112	5.4	2,200	118	5.4	4.9
Tennessee	7,065	533	7.6	7,927	606	7.6	7.9
Texas	18,386	699	3.8	19,632	849	4.3	12.0
Virginia	9,991	699	7.0	10,922	786	7.2	9.3
West Virginia	1,221	83	6.8	1,279	86	6.7	5.2
Total	105,302	6,080	5.8	113,277	7,080	6.3	12.5
Percent of total banking employment		21.8			22.1		
Percent of total Negro employment		24.9			23.2		

TABLE 18. (Continued)

Region and State	1967			1968			Percent Negro Share of Growth[a]
	All Employees	Negro	Percent Negro	All Employees	Negro	Percent Negro	
Northeast Region							
Connecticut	8,392	294	3.5	8,926	345	3.9	9.6
Maine	916	1	0.1	1,119	1	0.1	0.0
Massachusetts	15,590	385	2.5	16,093	490	3.0	20.9
New Hampshire	615	—	—	650	—	—	—
New Jersey	16,575	674	4.1	17,272	855	5.0	26.0
New York	91,530	7,410	8.1	97,262	9,748	10.0	40.8
Pennsylvania	26,763	940	3.5	29,187	1,364	4.7	17.5
Rhode Island	3,390	53	1.6	3,634	70	1.9	7.0
Vermont	457	—	—	484	—	—	—
Total	164,228	9,757	5.9	174,627	12,873	7.4	30.0
Percent of total banking employment	34.0			34.1			
Percent of total Negro employment	39.9			42.2			
North Central Region							
Illinois	28,370	2,113	7.4	30,163	2,395	7.9	15.7
Indiana	9,159	343	3.7	9,637	412	4.3	14.4
Iowa	2,895	42	1.5	3,048	39	1.3	*
Kansas	2,072	88	4.2	2,217	120	5.4	22.0
Michigan	21,665	1,165	5.4	22,690	1,627	7.2	45.1
Minnesota	5,590	96	1.7	5,875	94	1.6	*
Missouri	8,870	530	6.0	9,179	613	6.7	26.9
Nebraska	2,281	46	2.0	2,416	46	1.9	0.0

North Dakota	230	—	—	234	—	—	—
Ohio	22,414	1,095	4.9	23,260	1,312	5.6	25.7
South Dakota	863	—	—	870	—	—	—
Wisconsin	6,428	108	1.7	7,064	143	2.0	5.5
Total	110,837	5,626	5.1	116,653	6,801	5.8	20.2
Percent of total banking employment			22.9			22.8	
Percent of total Negro employment			23.0			22.3	
West Region							
Arizona	6,543	86	1.3	6,903	95	1.4	2.5
California	71,656	2,660	3.7	76,140	3,331	4.4	15.0
Colorado	4,798	93	1.9	4,956	109	2.2	10.1
Idaho	232	1	0.4	245	1	0.4	0.0
Montana	995	—	—	980	1	0.1	*
Nevada	1,694	17	1.0	1,649	28	1.7	*
New Mexico	1,165	5	0.4	1,149	11	1.0	*
Oregon	7,887	58	0.7	7,994	76	1.0	16.8
Utah	2,354	—	—	2,536	3	0.1	1.6
Washington	5,391	48	0.9	5,337	69	1.3	*
Wyoming	266	5	1.9	268	5	1.9	0.0
Total	102,981	2,973	2.9	108,157	3,729	3.4	14.6
Percent of total banking employment			21.3			21.1	
Percent of total Negro employment			12.2			12.2	

Source: Data in the author's possession.

a For Alabama, for example, 167 additional employees were added between the years, of which 55 were Negro. Therefore, 32.9 percent of all new employees added were Negro.

b These figures somewhat off as a result of one bank's figures being counted twice (for both Negro and white).

* Decrease in either total or Negro employment.

banking retraction in heavily Negro areas or cities, but at least
the situation is not quite so sensitive as is commonly supposed.

Upward Mobility

The slower Negro employment growth rate in the South region,
seen above, brings to mind the related question of whether there
is also a slower upward occupational mobility for Negroes in
banks in the South. Detailed regional employment breakdowns
by job category are not available for all banks, but our 1968
banking survey does indicate that this may be the case. Table
19 contains the aggregate employment data by race, sex, and job
classification for forty-six banks located throughout the country.
Table 20 presents the same information for the thirteen banks
included in the survey which are located in areas defined as
"southern" by the Bureau of the Census. These tables show that
although the thirteen southern banks have a total Negro proportion which is almost identical to the forty-six bank average, the
southern banks' average is made up more predominantly of blue
collar Negroes.

Southern banks do not need or have a greater proportion of
blue collar workers than banks elsewhere. The tables show that
southern banks are 4.5 percent blue collar compared with the
national aggregate 4.3 percent. Additionally, responses to a survey question on this point indicated that whereas about 28 percent of the southern banks do at least a significant amount of
their own building maintenance, 36 percent of banks outside the
South also perform this function. (The other banks contract
maintenance to outside organizations.)

POPULATION AND EMPLOYMENT

Measured by its total work force size of just under 800,000
persons in 1965, banking is one of the top twenty-five industries
in the country.[36] New York City, with about one-sixth of the
total employment, is very much the banking center of the nation,
but banks are distributed as cities are throughout the country,
wherever industry or commerce abounds. Even so, it is not a
uniform distribution. In 1966, banking was among the top fifteen industries in eleven states, according to the total industry

---

[36] U.S. Bureau of the Census, *Current Population Reports*, "Industrial
Characteristics of the Population," (Washington: U.S. Government Printing
Office, 1965).

TABLE 19. *The Banking Industry*
Employment by Race, Sex, and Occupational Group
46 Commercial Banks Surveyed
United States, 1968

Occupational Group	All Employees			Male			Female		
	Total	Negro	Percent Negro	Total	Negro	Percent Negro	Total	Negro	Percent Negro
Officials and managers	38,195	377	1.0	32,931	263	0.8	5,264	114	2.2
Professionals	7,073	120	1.7	5,533	101	1.8	1,540	19	1.2
Technicians	2,790	202	7.2	2,336	157	6.7	454	45	9.9
Sales workers	767	9	1.2	631	8	1.3	136	1	0.7
Office and clerical	147,921	14,166	9.6	32,835	3,246	9.9	115,086	10,920	9.5
Total white collar	196,746	14,874	7.6	74,266	3,775	5.1	122,480	11,099	9.1
Craftsmen	767	43	5.6	731	42	5.7	36	1	2.8
Operatives	1,924	297	15.4	1,510	180	11.9	414	117	28.3
Laborers and service workers	6,104	1,512	24.8	4,851	1,303	26.9	1,253	209	16.7
Total blue collar	8,795	1,852	21.1	7,092	1,525	21.5	1,703	327	19.2
Total	205,541	16,726	8.1	81,358	5,300	6.5	124,183	11,426	9.2

Source: Data in author's possession.

TABLE 20. *The Banking Industry*
Employment by Race, Sex, and Occupational Group
13 Commercial Banks Surveyed
South Region, 1968

Occupational Group	All Employees			Male			Female		
	Total	Negro	Percent Negro	Total	Negro	Percent Negro	Total	Negro	Percent Negro
Officials and managers	3,217	18	0.6	2,972	17	0.6	245	1	0.4
Professionals	883	8	0.9	712	4	0.6	171	4	2.3
Technicians	138	9	6.5	109	9	8.3	29	—	—
Sales workers	16	1	6.2	16	1	6.2	—	—	—
Office and clerical	13,283	993	7.5	2,900	297	10.2	10,383	696	6.7
Total white collar	17,537	1,029	5.9	6,709	328	4.9	10,828	701	6.5
Craftsmen	39	2	5.1	38	2	5.3	1	—	—
Operatives	37	19	51.4	35	19	54.3	2	—	—
Laborers and service workers	744	427	57.4	561	302	53.8	183	125	68.3
Total blue collar	820	448	54.6	634	323	50.9	186	125	67.2
Total	18,357	1,477	8.0	7,343	651	8.9	11,014	826	7.5

Source: Data in author's possession.

Note: Three additional Southern banks visited would release no data.

figures reported to the Equal Employment Opportunity Commission.[37]

Generally in these eleven states, the banking industry rated better as an employer of Negroes than as an employer. In other words, although other industries had larger work forces than banking, in most of these states banking had a larger proportion of both Negro white collar and Negro blue collar employees. In itself, this means very little. Consider one of the states, Idaho: there are so few Negroes in banking in Idaho that the percent Negro in the industry rounds off to zero. In fact, there is but a single Negro blue collar employee who was reported from the entire state. But his presence so affects the blue collar employment ratio that banking shows a higher proportion of Negro blue collar workers in the state than any other major industry.

Obviously, there are not many Negroes employed in Idaho; there are not many Negroes in Idaho. In Delaware, on the other hand, 41 percent of all blue collar employees in banking are Negro, but the industry rates only third among major state industries as an employer of blue collar Negroes. The real question is: In which state are banks being more responsive to the call for more Negro jobs?

It is not a bad initial assumption to suppose that Negro employment in banks is related to the Negro population ratio in areas near the bank. Obviously, there are more Negroes in the South than there are in the rest of the country as a proportion of the population, and on this basis, we should expect more Negro employees there. Figure 6 is a chart of Negro banking employment ratios (from 1966) and Negro population proportions (from the 1960 census) for individual states. This figure generally justifies the positive correlation between population and employment, but it must be carefully interpreted. The flaw which obscures the apparently obvious is that the correlations shown between overall Negro population and banking employment do not take into account the uneven distribution of banks.

Surely, there are more Negroes in any town chosen at random in Mississippi than there are in a town of equivalent size chosen at random in Wyoming. However, that fact is not par-

---

[37] These states are Arizona, California, Delaware, Idaho, Maine, Montana, Nevada, New York, Rhode Island, Vermont, and Washington. From Equal Employment Opportunity Commission, *Job Patterns for Minorities and Women in Private Industry, 1966*, Report No. 1 (Washington: The Commission, 1968), Part II, p. 124.

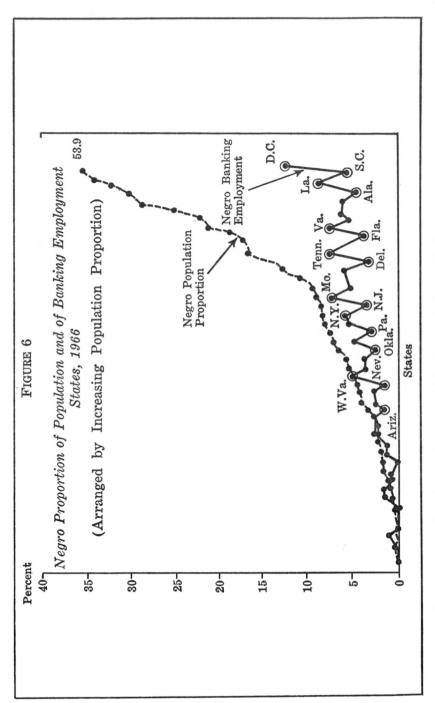

FIGURE 6

*Negro Proportion of Population and of Banking Employment
States, 1966*

(Arranged by Increasing Population Proportion)

Source: Negro banking employment, Table 17; population, 1960 Census.

ticularly germane. By and large, banking institutions, and especially the larger ones with which we are generally dealing in this study, are located in the urban areas of the country. It is therefore the Negro population proportion of individual urban areas that should be of concern rather than some state or broader region's overall Negro population—a population whose presence does not greatly affect the number of potential Negro job seekers.

City Population Figures

The cities whose banking data we shall investigate in this section are those which were selected by the author for personal visits during the Summer of 1968. There are seventeen cities which represent a reasonably good cross-section of the country, both geographically and sociologically. New York, Philadelphia, and Pittsburgh are all banking centers located in the industrial Northeast, and should provide good representation of that area. Similarly, Chicago, Detroit, and Cleveland were taken from the North Central region. The South and West, as areas of higher problem content, received proportionally higher coverage. In the South, banks were visited in the District of Columbia, Atlanta, Baltimore, Dallas, Richmond, and Winston-Salem.[38] In the western section of the country, banks were visited in Phoenix, Los Angeles, San Francisco, Denver, and Seattle.

For those and other major cities in the country, population data are available on two bases. The first is for the city itself, and the second for the "standard metropolitan statistical area" of which the city is the focus. Even in states which allow extensive branching, the greatest majority of the clerical, check clearing, and bookkeeping functions are located in the downtown offices. And even though some employees commute to the main office or are employed in the suburban branches, we feel the statistical base which should be used for examining the responsiveness of banks to any segment of the local population should be the city itself rather than the standard metropolitan statistical area. However, because of the heavy Negro concentration at the core of most major cities, the use of the central city population will tend to emphasize racial employment statistical discrepancies somewhat, and this point should be borne in mind.

---

[38] Reflecting our policy of not disclosing specific information on specific banking organizations, statistical data collected in Winston-Salem will not be presented in any tabulations where it would show alone, because its dominant banking institution would be too easily recognized.

TABLE 21. Total and Negro Population
United States and Selected Cities
1950-1970

City	1950 (Census)			1960 (Census)			1965 (Estimate)			1970 (Projection)		
	Total	Negro	Percent Negro	Total	Negro	Percent Negro	Total	Negro	Percent Negro	Total	Negro	Percent Negro
	(in thousands)											
United States Total	150,697	15,042	10	178,465	18,860	11	192,852	21,058	11	208,220	23,324	11
Atlanta	331	121	37	487	186	38	515	198	38	540	212	39
Baltimore	950	225	24	939	326	35	930	378	41	920	432	47
Chicago	3,621	492	14	3,550	813	23	3,600	960	27	3,610	1,150	32
Cleveland	915	148	16	876	251	29	811	277	34	805	305	38
Dallas	434	57	13	680	129	19	740	165	22	800	200	25
Denver	416	15	4	494	30	6	502	40	8	510	51	10
Detroit	1,850	301	16	1,670	482	29	1,650	650	39	1,700	800	47
Los Angeles	1,970	171	9	2,479	335	14	2,750	500	18	3,000	700	23
New York City	7,892	748	9	7,782	1,088	14	8,282	1,300	16	8,100	1,500	19
Philadelphia	2,072	376	14	2,003	529	26	2,070	610	29	2,200	700	32
Phoenix	107	5	5	439	21	5	520	40	8	600	60	10
Pittsburgh	677	82	12	604	101	17	607	115	19	610	126	21
Richmond	230	73	32	220	92	42	215	101	47	215	110	51
San Francisco	775	44	6	740	74	10	740	100	14	750	126	17
Seattle	468	16	3	557	27	5	602	40	7	647	56	9
Washington (D.C.)	802	281	38	764	412	54	801	506	63	840	574	68
16 City Total	23,510	3,155	13	24,284	4,896	20	25,335	5,980	24	25,847	7,102	27

Source: The Center for Research in Marketing, Inc., The Negro Population: 1965 Estimates and 1970 Projections (Peekskill, New York: The Corporation, 1966).

The population data for the cities which we shall investigate are given in Table 21. Census population is provided for 1950 and 1960, and estimates and projections of the population for 1965 and 1970 are also included.[39]

It is the exceptional city in the table which will not show about double the Negro population of 1950 by 1970. It is obvious from the table that the often-mentioned net in-migration of Negroes to the cities is very much a reality. In 1940 (not shown) the Negro population proportion of these sixteen cities was actually less than that for the country as a whole. It will be two and one-half times as great by 1970, when it is estimated that 12.4 percent of the total population of the country and 30.4 percent of the Negro population will be living in them. Their populations are increasingly composed of youngsters who flock to them to seek education, to find challenging employment, or simply to be "where the action is."

All of these factors are reflected in banking employment. Population, mobility, and youth have contributed greatly to the high turnover rates with which banks must contend. The rapidly increasing numbers of Negroes in the cities means that banks, as major urban employers, must be especially responsive to the needs of this segment of the population. It also means that these banks must be prepared to modify their viewpoints and policies for internal structuring, expansion, customer relations, and loan policies, among other factors, to reflect the new realities, and to appeal to the employability and growing affluence of Negro citizens.

Negro Banking Employment, Sixteen Selected Cities

Table 22 shows the degree to which banks in our sample cities have responded to the call for increased Negro employment. Between the two comparable years, 1967 and 1968, considerable growth is evident. These are entirely "comparable" years, as data are included only from those firms for which information was available in both years. Therefore, the growth results from expansion alone and not from including additional or different firms. On the average, one employee in twelve was Negro, an average which is quite clearly beyond the "hire the handicapped," or "showcase Negro" stage but still very short of matching the

---

[39] The Center for Research in Marketing, Inc., *The Negro Population: 1965 Estimates and 1970 Projections* (Peekskill, New York: The Corporation, 1966).

TABLE 22. The Banking Industry
Employment by Race
Selected Cities, 1966-1968

City	1966			1967			1968			1967-1968 Percent Negro Share of Growth
	All Employees	Negro	Percent Negro	All Employees	Negro	Percent Negro	All Employees	Negro	Percent Negro	
United States Total	376,017	16,561	4.4	483,348	24,436	5.1	512,714	30,483	6.0	20.6
Atlanta	5,174	333	6.4	6,385	436	6.8	6,865	529	7.7	19.4
Baltimore	6,449	423	6.6	4,626	314	6.8	4,915	351	7.1	12.8
Chicago	19,947	989	5.0	17,182	1,547	9.0	18,728	1,774	9.5	14.7
Cleveland	4,092	128	3.1	7,536	462	6.1	7,849	533	6.8	22.7
Dallas	3,408	82	2.4	4,173	172	4.1	4,803	197	4.1	4.0
Denver	2,498	62	2.5	3,198	73	2.3	3,355	91	2.7	11.5
Detroit	11,360	854	7.5	9,447	885	9.4	10,016	1,271	12.7	67.8
Los Angeles	10,396	577	5.6	15,139	795	5.3	16,065	922	5.7	13.7
New York City	68,744	4,380	6.4	67,286	6,953	10.3	72,071	9,057	12.6	44.0
Philadelphia	7,115	300	4.2	13,260	746	5.6	14,545	1,088	7.5	26.6
Phoenix	4,073	65	1.6	5,863	79	1.3	6,120	85	1.4	2.3
Pittsburgh	6,300	147	2.3	2,763	60	2.2	3,072	72	2.3	3.9
Richmond	2,290	188	8.2	4,423	356	8.0	6,095	471	7.7	6.9
San Francisco	13,385	633	4.7	50,348	1,802	3.6	53,224	2,322	4.4	18.1
Seattle	3,146	35	1.1	3,296	35	1.1	3,082	53	1.7	—
Washington, (D.C.)	2,639	322	12.2	4,053	653	16.1	4,310	805	18.7	59.1
16 City Total	171,016	9,518	5.6	218,978	15,368	7.0	235,115	19,621	8.3	26.4

Source: Data in author's possession.

city population ratios. Three out of every ten employees added during 1967 by the 172 banks which make up this sample were Negro. This is a bit higher than the average population ratio of 25 percent for the same cities as interpolated from Table 21, yet the breakdowns for individual cities show some problem areas.

Negro Share in Employment Growth, Sixteen Selected Cities

The Negro share in employment growth, shown in the last column of Table 22 illustrates the best approximation we have for a Negro hiring rate. If we can make the assumption that Negro and non-Negro turnover rates are the same, then this column shows the net gain in Negro employment in 1968 over 1967. This gain compared with the overall bank employment expansion in the city gives what would be, roughly, the Negro hiring ratio. There is a general sort of correlation between the two visible in the figure, but it does not hold when the percentage growth overall is compared with Negro participation in growth. In other words, it is not the fastest growing banks which are hiring the greatest proportion of new Negroes (which would tend to support an argument that in a highly competitive, tight labor market Negroes fare better) but rather the largest banks (or at least banks in cities in which banking is an important industry employing many persons) which are hiring the greatest proportion of Negroes.

Measures of Status and Growth

Our data do not relate employment growth to population change. The 22.7 percent participation of Negroes in employment growth in Cleveland, for example, shows how well Negroes did there compared to whites. But it does not answer the question of how well they *should* have done. Although we do not suggest it as a normative standard for measuring the sufficiency of Negro employment, a benchmark used by many is the population proportion. Under it, the measure of the status of the industry's response would take the form of a comparison between the number of Negroes who would have been hired, had hiring been done along strictly racial lines, and the number who were hired in actuality. There are serious arguments against the use of this measure as a standard, so it should be remembered that we are using this comparison as *one* benchmark rather than *the* standard.

There were 29,366 more people reported working in banking in 1968 than in 1967. At that time, the country had a population ratio slightly above 11 percent Negro, and so if hiring had been done then on racial lines some 3,200 of the new employees would be black. Actually, 6,047 were Negro, and so banks in the aggregate were hiring at a substantially higher than "ratial parity" rate. However, because neither banks nor Negroes are uniformly distributed throughout the country, this overall experience is not reflected equally in the individual cities.

The results of producing similar calculations for regions and individual cities are in Table 23, "measure of status." Only Detroit, of the North Central region, shows a hiring surplus and the net for the three sample cities in the region is negative, indicating a hiring deficit. Yet the overall North Central region shows a surplus. This is in keeping with our findings, and reflects the fact that the region's Negroes are located in a few major cities. A very striking thing in the table is the size of the hiring surplus generated by New York City banks. Alone, this city's banks account for nearly 50 percent of the country's total surplus. Less hopeful are the figures for Richmond and Washington (although see the note on the table for Richmond).

Finally in this series is the "measure of growth" column in Table 23. This column shows that in the country as a whole, every region of the country, and thirteen of sixteen survey cities, Negro participation in employment growth between 1967 and 1968 was higher than the level of Negro employment had been in 1967. The table is self-explanatory.

Again in this instance, the most positive figures are those from New York City. In fact, from all of the tables and figures in this section, New York City can be seen as not only the banking center of the nation, but also as the center for Negro employment.

ORGANIZATIONAL SIZE

In the last section and several times previously in this study there have been strong indications that the most powerful influence on the receptiveness of banking organizations to Negro employees is organizational size. Dr. Andrew Brimmer, a member of the Board of Governors of the Fedeal Reserve System, asked the Equal Employment Opportunity Commission to prepare a

TABLE 23. *The Banking Industry*
Measures of Status and Growth in Negro Employment
United States, Regions, and Selected Cities
1967-1968

Locality	Increase in number of Negro employees 1967-1968	Measure of Status		Measure of Growth	
		Increase expected if hired in ratio to area population (1965 base)	Hiring surplus or (deficit)	Increase expected if hired in ratio to 1967 employment	Hiring surplus or (deficit)
United States Total	6,047	3,230	2,817	1,498	4,549
South Region	1,000	1,595	(595)	463	537
Northeast Region	3,116	832	2,284	614	2,502
North Central Region	1,175	465	710	297	878
West Region	756	207	549	150	606
Atlanta	93	182	(89)	33	60
Baltimore	37	118	(81)	20	17
Chicago	227	417	(190)	139	88
Cleveland	71	106	(35)	19	52
Dallas	25	139	(114)	26	(1)
Denver	18	13	5	4	14
Detroit	386	222	164	53	333
Los Angeles	127	167	(40)	49	78
New York City	2,104	766	1,338	493	1,611
Philadelphia	342	373	(31)	72	270
Phoenix	6	21	(11)	3	3
Pittsburgh	12	59	(47)	7	5
Richmond [a]	115	786	(671)	134	(19)
San Francisco	520	403	117	104	416
Seattle	18	(15)	33	—[b]	—
Washington, D.C.	152	162	(10)	41	111
16 City Total	4,253	3,873	380	1,130	3,123

Source: Tables 18, 21, and 22.

[a] Richmond: Major portion of growth in Richmond came through merger rather than "new hiring."

[b] Banking total employment decreased between 1967 and 1968.

Calculations as follows:

Increase in total employment (1967-1968) times Negro population proportion of city or area (1965) yields "Increase Expected if Hired in Ratio to Area Population." This minus actual 1967-1968 Negro employment increase yields "Hiring Surplus or (Deficit)."

Increase in total employment (1967-1968) times 1967 Negro employment ratio yields "Increase Expected if Hired in Ratio to 1967 Employment." This minus actual 1967-1968 Negro employment increase yields "Hiring Surplus or (Deficit)."

special tabulation by bank size from the 1966 EEOC data.[40] A synopsis of that tabulation is included here as Figure 7.[41]

The distribution seen in the figures shows that the 216 largest banks in the sample, 12.6 percent of the total number of banks had over 60 percent of the employment population, and almost 70 percent of the Negroes. Thus there are not only more Negroes but also a higher proportion of Negroes in the larger institutions.[42]

Confirming these results are our own calculations from the 1966 field survey of 738 banks. Included there were seventy banks reporting a total employment of over 1,000 persons each. The average Negro employment percentage for this group of the largest banks was 4.8 simple (adding the percentages reported by individual banks and dividing by seventy) and 5.5 weighted. Because the weighted average is larger than the simple, the indication is that the very largest of the large banks are also showing the highest Negro proportions.

Because very few large banks exist anywhere except in large cities—and therefore near the greatest Negro concentrations— the locational factor might bear greater weight than the size. To illustrate that this is not the case, we have included Table 24 which shows the banking employment distribution by size of reporting unit in Chicago and New York City. These distributions are based on 1968 employment totals for all of the banks (not "reporting units") in each city which reported figures during both 1967 and 1968. Forty-five banks were included in this category

---

[40] From: Special Tabulation by Equal Employment Opportunity Commission, in: Andrew F. Brimmer, *Employment Patterns and the Quest for Equal Opportunity in Banking*, A Report Before a Conference on Bank Employment Practices, Sponsored by U.S. Treasury Department and the Michigan Human Relations Commission, Lansing, Michigan, May 22, 1968 (Washington: Board of Governors of the Federal Reserve System, 1968), Table 4.

[41] The total employment figure for the industry of 509,214 does not agree with any other 1966 total which we have seen from EEOC. However, the difference is not so great as to cause significant statistical differences.

[42] This result may be over-emphasized by one continuing point of confusion involving the differentiation of "firms" and "reporting units." The data for 1966 is almost invariably based on reporting units rather than firms, and we assume that to have been the case here. The numerical distributions by size of "firm" are therefore skewed to the "under 100," and "100-250" categories, since many of the "firms" recorded there are branches which, presumably, would tend to reflect the employment policies of the home office. On the other hand, insofar as these branches of large (over 500 employees) banks tend to be "white, suburban" branches, the statistical effect is to understate the Negro employment proportion of the smallest banks and overstate it for the largest banks.

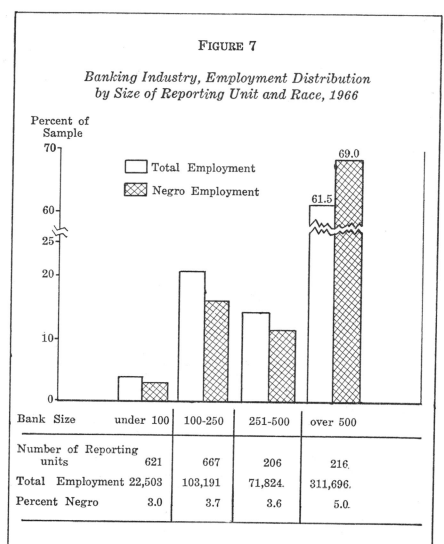

FIGURE 7

Banking Industry, Employment Distribution
by Size of Reporting Unit and Race, 1966

Bank Size	under 100	100-250	251-500	over 500
Number of Reporting units	621	667	206	216.
Total Employment	22,503	103,191	71,824.	311,696.
Percent Negro	3.0	3.7	3.6	5.0.

Notes: (1) The "Under 100" Column was derived as a residual.

(2) Size criterion for classification was "reporting unit" in EEOC tabulation, not total firm size.

Source: Andrew F. Brimmer, *Employment Patterns and the Quest for Equal Opportunity in Banking*, a Report Before a Conference on Bank Employment Practices Sponsored by U.S. Treasury Department and Michigan Human Relations Commission, Lansing, Michigan, May 22, 1968 (Washington: Board of Governors of the Federal Reserve System, 1968), Table 4.

in Chicago, ranging in size from 51 to 6,416 employees. In New York City, where branch banking is allowed, the number of banks included is smaller, but the average size of the banks is larger. All of the banks in each of the cities are facing the same Negro population proportions. The correlation between increasing size and increasing percentage Negro employment is obvious from the table.

The only surprise in the table comes from Chicago where the Negro employment proportion for banks with under one hundred employees is greater than for banks with between 100 and 250 employees. Here it should be remembered that the absolute sizes we are dealing with are very small, and under these circumstances, the presence of a very few Negroes will greatly affect percentage results.

TABLE 24. *The Banking Industry*
Employment by Size of Reporting Unit
Chicago and New York City
1968

	Bank Size (by total employment)[a]			
	Under 100	100-250	251-500	Over 500
Chicago				
Number of Reporting Units	18	15	6	6
Total Employment	1,403	2,249	1,756	13,320
Negro Employment	80	67	119	1508
Percent Negro	5.7	3.0	6.8	11.3
New York City				
Number of Reporting Units	1	17	6	9
Total Employment	87	2,749	2,000	67,235
Negro Employment	4	226	167	8,660
Percent Negro	4.6	8.2	8.4	12.9

Source: Data in the author's possession.

Note: [a] This distribution is based on 1968 employment totals for all banks in the respective cities for which employment data was available for both 1967 and 1968.

Analysis of the Influence of Size

A number of factors explain why the scale factor is so important to Negro employment in banking. The very smallest banks, ranging in size up to perhaps seventy or seventy-five employees, are essentially in the "family enterprise" stage, in that the president and officers of the firm can know all of the employees by name. Frequently, organizations of this size are highly paternalistic, and the desire may exist to perpetuate a closely-knit employment structure if one exists. This may operate to the exclusion of Negroes except in "traditional" jobs.

In organizations of this size and slightly larger, personnel men may hesitate to add Negroes to the staff for fear of not knowing how to handle racial problems which might arise. A higher proportion of personnel men on this level will be inexperienced with Negro employees, and unfamiliar with the nuances of the equal employment legislation.

The largest banking organizations are able to attract the best managerial talent, and are able to afford sophisticated personnel functions. For example, a number of large banks have established separate "compliance" sections which specialize entirely in activities related to equal employment. Additionally, better communications exist among the largest banks in any given area, and therefore, to a much greater degree than in smaller institutions, personnel men can learn from each others' experiences how to handle problems related to Negro employees.

Another factor in operation in the largest banks tending to increase their Negro proportions is the organizational flexibility associated with large size. Larger institutions can afford not only the facilities, teachers, and materials necessary for extensive training programs, but also can afford the payroll costs of nonproductive trainees for longer periods of time. As a result, the larger institutions can accept persons for employment with lower levels of skill development—and many Negroes are still in this category.

Finally, the very largest banks have both more entry-level jobs —because of their more than proportionately larger paperwork flow—and more Negro applicants.

DECENTRALIZATION

Those states which do not allow branch banking necessarily have a more decentralized banking structure than states which do allow branch offices. We have not produced any direct statistics on the effect of decentralization on Negro employment levels because of the difficulties involved in separating out locational factors and other influences on the statistical results. However, branch office hiring is generally under tight personnel control from the home offices, if hiring is done in the branches at all. Therefore, following the statistical trends above, we would expect to find a higher proportion of Negro employees in a branch office than in an independent bank of the same size.

Our 1968 survey shows that branches do indeed reflect the personnel policies of the home offices. Thirty-nine of the banks visited are located in states which allow branch banking. In twenty-two of those thirty-nine all of the hiring for the entire branch network is done by the main office (or occasionally two main offices). In an additional eleven banks, all of the hiring is done at the main office except for that done for a few far-flung branches. Only four of the thirty-nine banks reported all clerical branch hiring to be done by the individual branches (under home office policy control); in two cases, individual departments in the main offices as well as branches were reported able either to do their own hiring or to utilize the main office as a "hiring service" if desired.

NON-NEGRO RACIAL MINORITIES

One factor affecting the level of employment of Negroes in banking may be the competition afforded them by members of other racial minorities. Our almost exclusive concern in this study has been with Negroes, because they constitute by far the largest of the racial minorities. Members of larger religious and ethnic groups are not as visible and therefore presumably, not as "discriminatable." [43] Members of the smaller racial minori-

---

[43] The American Jewish Committee might, with some cause, dispute this statement. In a survey of the nation's fifty leading commercial banks conducted in about 1965, the Committee found that only 1.3 percent of the banks' senior officers (the top ranking officials listed in the institutions' annual reports) and 0.9 percent of middle management executives (down through the vice-presidential bracket) were Jewish. In New York City Jews make up nearly one-quarter of the population and about half of the college graduates. (From: *Patterns of Exclusion from the Executive Suite: Commercial Banking*, The American Jewish Committee, Institute of Human Relations, New York: By The Institute, 1966, p. 2-3.)

ties tend to be found in numerical concentration in only a few cities or in regional enclaves where there local difficulties are best dealt with locally. Nevertheless, it is instructive to get some feeling for the comparative position of Negroes in banking with respect to the other recognized minorities.

Some data are available from the Equal Employment Opportunity Commission on the relative participation rates in banking of the various recognized minority groups (Negroes, Spanish Surnamed Americans, Orientals, and American Indians).[44] The EEOC presents only employment data. The most recent population data available for minority groups (except Negroes) comes from the 1960 census. At that time, there were about 18.9 million Negroes; 3.7 million Mexican Americans; 890,000 Puerto Ricans; 520,000 American Indians; 464,000 Japanese; 237,000 Chinese; and 176,000 Filipinos.[45] Some appropriate comparisons are found in Table 25.

Employment data for Negroes can often be utilized as indicative of the situation for minority groups generally, but Table 25 shows this not to be entirely the case in banking. Although Negroes make up 76 percent of all of the recognized minorities, they are only 56 percent of the minority employment in banks. Whatever discrimination against minorities by banks these figures reflect, therefore, is either in greater effect against Negroes (and American Indians) or in lesser effect against Spanish Surnamed Americans, and considerably diminished effect against Orientals (who are seen from the table to be positively preferred by bankers).

Another way to look at this is as follows: (We are mixing 1960 population data and 1966 banking data here, so caution is recommended in the use of the absolute numbers.) Of the 179,-323,000 people in the country, 510,875 were in banking, or one person of every 351 of the general population; similarly, one of every 614 minority persons was in banking; one of every 835 Negroes; one of every 364 Spanish Surnamed Americans; one of every 179 Orientals; and one of every 1210 American Indians. Here it is seen that Spanish Americans participate in banking to about the same degree as does the overall population, Orientals to a much higher degree, and the other groups to a much lesser degree.

---

[44] U.S. Equal Employment Opportunity Commission, Report No. 1, *Job Patterns for Minorities and Women in Private Industry, 1966*, Part I (Washington: The Commission, 1968).

[45] *U.S. Census of Population, 1960*, Vol. 1.

TABLE 25. The Banking Industry
Negro Employment Compared with Employment of Other Minorities
United States, 1966

	Population (1960)	Banking Population (1966)	Percentage Distribution			
			Population	Banking population	Minority population	Banking minority population
Total population	179,323,000	510,875	100.0	100.0	—	—
Total recognized minorities	24,863,000	40,493	13.9	8.0	100.0	100.0
Negroes	18,872,000	22,581	10.5	4.4	75.9	55.8
Spanish surnamed Americans	4,590,000	12,587	2.6	2.5	18.5	31.1
Mexican Americans	3,700,000					
Puerto Ricans	890,000					
Orientals	877,000	4,892	0.5	1.0	3.5	12.1
Japanese	464,000					
Chinese	237,000					
Filipinos	176,000					
American Indians	524,000	433	0.3	0.1	2.1	1.0

Source: Population Data: U.S. Census of Population, 1960, Vol. I.

Banking Data : U.S. Equal Employment Opportunity Commission, Job Patterns for Minorities and Women in Private Industry - 1966, Report No. 1 (Washington: The Commission, 1968), Part I, p. C44.

Insofar as locational considerations are a factor, the plight of the American Indians, who are heavily concentrated in non-populous and generally bankless regions of the Southwest and Far West, becomes somewhat more understandable, if no less real. But there is no ready explanation, on racial or locational terms, for the industry's affinity for Orientals.

If attenion is directed to internal job classifications, the diversity of experience of the different minority groups becomes even more apparent, as seen in Table 26.

Note that even though the Oriental population is miniscule compared with Negro population in the country, there were almost twice as many Oriental officers and managers in banking in 1966. A similar situation exists (although to a lesser degree) for Spanish Surnamed Americans.

TABLE 26. *The Banking Industry*
Minority Group Employment by Occupational Classification
United States, 1966

| Minority Group | All Employees | Occupational Classification | | | | |
| | | White Collar | | | | Blue Collar |
		Total	Officers and managers	Clerical workers	Other	
		Number of Employees				
All Employees	510,875	478,604	88,107	373,251	17,246	32,271
Negroes	22,581	14,762	343	14,080	339	7,819
Spanish Surnamed Americans	12,587	11,860	762	10,869	229	727
Orientals	4,892	4,771	655	3,944	172	121
American Indians	433	411	64	334	13	22
		Percentage Distribution				
All Employees	100.0	93.7	17.3	73.1	3.4	6.3
Negroes	100.0	65.4	1.5	62.4	1.5	34.6
Spanish Surnamed Americans	100.0	94.2	6.1	86.3	1.8	5.8
Orientals	100.0	97.5	13.4	80.6	3.5	2.5
American Indians	100.0	94.9	14.8	77.1	3.0	5.1

Source: U. S. Equal Employment Opportunity Commission, *Job Patterns for Minorities and Women in Private Industry, 1966*, Report No. 1 (Washington: The Commission, 1968), Part I, p. C44.

The second part of the table is simply a percentage distribution by job category for each minority group. Once employed in banking, minority group members except Negroes hold jobs distributed about the organization to about the same degree as "anybody else." Although the proportion of officers and managers of all of the minority groups is somewhat lower than the overall proportion, the Negro proportion is very much lower. The distribution of American Indian employment is somewhat surprising on the high side.

As a final index of the relative positions of the various minority groups in banking, Table 27 has been calculated. The banking population of each group in the occupational categories used is taken from Table 26. If minority group members were employed in banking in the same ratio as they were members of the national population, we could find the expected banking population of each by multiplying the "percent of population" (from Table 25) by the total banking employment (510,875 used here). Spanish Surnamed Americans, for example, are 2.6 percent of the population of the country. With perfect distribution of jobs among races, we would expect 2.6 percent of the 510,875 jobs in the banking industry, or 13,283, to be held by members of this group. The actual count shows 12,587, leaving a variance of 696 jobs. This variance is the number of persons who would have to be hired by the industry (or fired, if the variance were negative) in order for the industry to show the same racial distribution as the country does. (The fact that we are using 1960 population data affects the outcome only insofar as the racial *mix* of the population changed in the five intervening years; the change for the country as a whole during that period is not estimated to be significant.)

By similar logic, the occupational classification breakdown of all employees in banking in 1966 was taken as a benchmark, and racial variances were calculated for each job type. These variances are in Table 27.

The table makes it clear that if we are to be concerned about the lack of employment of minority group members in the banking industry the real problem is with respect to Negroes. Orientals are overemployed in every major category except blue collar; the Spanish American experience is mixed. American Indians are underemployed in clerical positions, but not to the same degree or even the same order of magnitude as are Negroes.

TABLE 27. *The Banking Industry*
Numerical Variances by Occupational Classification and
Minority Group
1966

| | | Job Classification | | | | |
| | | White Collar | | | | |
Minority Group	All Employees	Total	Officers and managers	Clerical workers	Other	Blue Collar
All Employees	0	0	0	0	0	0
Negroes	31,061	35,492	8,908	25,112	1,472	—4,431
Spanish Surnamed Americans	696	584	1,529	—1,164	219	112
Orientals	—2,338	—2,378	—214	—2,078	—86	40
American Indians	1,100	1,025	200	786	39	75

Source and explanation: See text.

Some feelings have been reported to exist on the part of non-Negro minority group members that, because of the national attention being devoted to Negroes specifically, the other minority group members were suffering from unfair competition.[46] If we look back at Tables 10 and 25, we can see that between 1966 and 1968 Negro employment proportions not only increased absolutely, but also increased with respect to total minority employment (61.5 percent compared to 55.8 percent for the earlier employment year).[47] But the two tables also show that the total minority proportion increased as well, from 8.0 percent to 9.1 percent. This indicates that although Negroes were being hired at a faster rate, the other minority group members were also being given increased representation in banking.

CONCLUSIONS

In general, this chapter has been devoted to analyzing the effect which the structure of the banking industry has upon the

---

[46] Interview, July 1968.

[47] Bear in mind that two different statistical series are being used here.

level of its Negro employment. We have sought here to analyze the reasons for the wide variation in employment levels reported by banks in different areas of the country, by banks of various sizes, and under varying degrees of central control.

In pursuing the analysis, we found some interesting results and also some surprising ones. We found, for example, that the cliche: "Nothing is going on in the South" is only partially true. Negroes are actually being employed by banks in the South at a rate which is proportionally greater than that seen in most other areas of the country. On the other hand, we found that, once employed, Negroes in the South apparently face a somewhat more restricted job horizon than they do in other areas. We found that the location of a banking institution by area of the country is not as important as is commonly supposed because, by and large, Negroes who are potentially job applicants to the banking industry live in the urban areas from which the majority of banking employment is drawn. The Negro population of these areas has little relationship to that of the state or region in which they are located.

Examining the data from individual cities, we did not find as close a correlation as we had expected between Negro population proportions and employment levels. We did find, however, that the banking industry in New York City comes closer than that in any other which we investigated to hiring Negroes and non-Negroes in the ratio which the relative population figures would indicate. This is important for several reasons. In the first place, the banking industry in New York City alone employs approximately 10 percent of the total work force of the industry. Secondly, the banking industry in New York City is actually adding Negroes to its work force at a rate which is greater than the population figures would lead us to expect. Thirdly, the banks in New York City, as the collective financial center of the country, are in a better position to communicate their Negro employment policies and experiences to banks located in other areas. The major institutions in the city are among the largest in the country, and therefore are able to afford, economically and organizationally, the experimentation necessary in the personnel function to develop the most effective procedures for molding large numbers of Negroes into their work forces.

The effect of organizational size on Negro employment levels was found to be greater than it is generally considered to be. We feel that there is a combination of factors bringing about this result: More Negroes apply to the larger banks; the banks themselves have had more experience with Negroes on the work force, are more sophisticated in their understanding of the entry-level Negroes' motivations, aspirations, and behavior patterns, and they are better able to afford special training and other personnel activities which might be required.

Finally, in this chapter, we investigated the experiences of Negroes in banking compared with those of other racial minority group members, and found that Negroes are underrepresented in the banking industry even compared with other minority group members. Although both groups are being hired at an increasing rate, Negroes are making up a larger and larger share of the total minority employment in the industry.

CHAPTER VI

External Influences

Of the external influences at work affecting Negro employment levels in banks, the major one is undoubtedly that which has emanated from the regulatory efforts of various government agencies. However, these regulatory efforts could not have been effective were it not for the prosperity and general upward trend in the state of the American economy over the past several years, which has allowed the creation of new jobs and permitted some personnel experimentation; additionally, these regulatory efforts might have been very different had it not been for the social pressures of NAACP, CORE, and others in the years preceding national legislation.

SOCIAL PRESSURES

The banking industry was relatively free from the forms of demonstrations practiced by the Negro social pressure organizations during the early 1960's. Such sit-ins and picketing as did occur before banks became subject to Executive Order 11246 in late 1966 were generally in support of demands for increased Negro employment. A sampling of the news media reveals that such picketing was carried on by the National Association for the Advancement of Colored People in East St. Louis in August of 1963,[48] and in Detroit during the same year.[49] During May of 1964, the Congress of Racial Equality conducted massive sit-ins and business disruptions in San Francisco to support increased Negro hiring. Included as a target of CORE's "harrassing techniques" were the San Francisco branches of the Bank of America, the country's largest bank, which had recently been commended by the California Fair Employment Practice Com-

---

[48] "Lay-Downs' at Bank," *New York Times*, August 13, 1963; "Bank Protest Barred," *New York Times*, August 17, 1963.

[49] "NAACP picketing of Detroit S & L halted as board pledges to weigh demand," *Business Week*, October 14, 1963, p. 38.

mission for its hiring of minorities.[50] In 1965, the NAACP in one instance added a call for a general boycott by Negroes and white sympathizers of a small savings and loan association which it was picketing.[51]

With the inclusion of banks under federal regulations prohibiting discrimination in employment,[52] organized social pressures began to take on a slightly different form. Not only did the form of the pressures change, but the organizations promoting them were generally different. In December 1966, an organization known as the Committee of Conscience Against Apartheid alleged that its members had withdrawn at least $23,112,190 from two major New York City banks as the opening stage of a boycott protesting the banks' involvement in the economy of South Africa.[53] Early in 1967, the City of New York announced its intention to use the city treasury as a social instrument in helping depressed neighborhoods by choosing as depositaries to hold city money "ghetto" neighborhood banks that agreed to help finance small business enterprises in their areas.[54]

In June of 1967, through the State Treasurer, Adlai Stevenson, III, the State of Illinois issued an order prohibiting the depositing of state funds in banks which discriminated in providing mortgage funds or other banking services. The primary thrust of this action was said to be "setting a needed precedent in breaking the 'gentlemen's agreement' among bankers and the real open-occupancy financing." [55]

---

[50] "Race Issues Rife in San Francisco," *New York Times*, May 22, 1964; "Who's to Decide if a Banker is 'Biased'?" *Business Week*, June 13, 1964, p. 29.

[51] "NAACP Continues Picketing at Suburb & Co.," *Philadelphia Tribune*, August 14, 1965; "NAACP Halts Picketing at Collingdale," *Evening Bulletin* (Philadelphia), Sept. 8, 1965.

[52] "President Issues Rules to Bar Bias in Banks," *Sunday Bulletin* (Philadelphia), August 28, 1966.

[53] "Boycott Is Pushed Against 2 Banks," *Evening Bulletin* (Philadelphia), December 7, 1966; "Editors Battling Apartheid," New Pittsburgh Courier, December 10, 1966.

[54] "City to Favor Banks Aiding Ghetto Firms," *New York Times*, January 12, 1967.

[55] "Stevenson Raps Banks Over Bias," *New Pittsburg Courier*, June 24, 1967.

Churchmen,[56] government officials,[57] banking associations,[58] and bankers themselves [59] have all joined in urging other bankers not only to improve the employment opportunities for Negroes, but also to become involved in helping to meet urban crises by providing low-cost funds for Negro housing projects or business undertakings. The calls for improved employment opportunity for Negroes since 1966 have generally taken the form of exhortations by individuals connected with Negro social pressure groups rather than by mass actions by the groups themselves.[60]

The progression of social pressures as seen above, although not an exhaustive account of the activities which have taken place, is representative of their general direction. Prior to 1966, they generally took the form of direct pressures such as sit-ins or other harassing techniques and were conducted by the Negro advancement organizations. The goal was to promote the hiring of Negroes into responsible jobs in the banking industry. Since 1966, when the banking industry became subject to more powerful federal regulation on discrimination in hiring, the primary goal of social action groups seems to have shifted away from employment and toward urban involvement. Sit-ins and harassments have generally given way to speeches and exhortations by both individuals and a wide range of organizations.

If the trends in social pressures on the banking industry continue in the indicated directions, and there is no reason to suppose that they will not, then the banking industry will have to be very careful over the next few years in defining the limits of its involvement in social responsibility for it is clear that those limits will be tested. We shall see in Chapter VIII that banks themselves (at least the large, urban ones) have already undertaken numerous social activities beyond providing employment.

---

[56] "Episcopalians Put $720,000 in Negro Banks," *New Pittsburgh Courier*, October 26, 1968.

[57] "Ghetto Lending Urged on Bankers," *New York Times*, November 11, 1967.

[58] "Ghettos Need Bank Loans, Lending Officials Are Told," *Evening Bulletin* (Philadelphia), March 4, 1969.

[59] "Banks Urged To Help Meet Urban Crises," *Evening Bulletin* (Philadelphia), October 21, 1968.

[60] "Bankers Urged To Help Ease Racial Tension," *Evening Bulletin* (Philadelphia), October 17, 1967; "Negro Leader Assails Bankers on Ghettos at Conference Here," *Philadelphia Inquirer*, October 30, 1968.

Union Pressures

Another form of external social pressure which might be thought to influence Negro employment levels is that provided by unions. Unions are usually considered to have a modifying effect on managerial prerogatives in hiring Negro employees. This aspect of union pressure, of course, can have at most a miniscule effect on an industry as little unionized as is the banking industry. There is, however, another point with respect to unions which is of concern to banking personnel managers—the converse of the effect of unions on Negro employment—and that is the effect of Negroes on the unionization of banks.

Twenty-two of forty-seven banks included in the author's survey were questioned as to the feelings of the bank personnel manager on whether Negro employees would have more of a tendency to support a union's organization attempt in the bank than would their white counterparts. The responses provide little in the way of direction. Five banks felt their Negro employees would be more inclined to support a unionization attempt, five felt they would be less inclined, nine felt there would be no difference between white and Negro employees, and three preferred not to express an opinion.

However, only two banks could speak authoritatively on the subject, having undergone a unionization attempt subsequent to the time when they had hired a significant number of Negroes. In those instances, the banks reported that Negro employees were, in the words of one, "against the union all the way." [61] The evidence of these two banks may countermand the fears felt by other banking managements which have not experienced an actual organizational attempt. It suggests that unionization and Negro employment are at least independent situations in the banking industry.

BROAD ECONOMIC TRENDS

As of the Spring of 1969, the American economy continues to be in the throes of an unparalleled expansion and a continuing period of prosperity. This particular period of prosperity began before Negroes were hired by the banking industry in any numbers. Although some economists fear that the rate of growth of the economy is decreasing and a mild recession may be in

---

[61] Interview, August 1968.

store sometime during the next two or three years, it is obvious
that the banking industry has not had the opportunity to test
its personnel policies with respect to Negroes in a recessionary
period.

In most industries, Negroes are considered to be the "last
hired, first fired." Many researchers therefore fear the sociological consequences of a recession on the Negro community. Evidence relating to this point in the banking industry is scant.
But we did have some indication in the last chapter that when
four Western states suffered a contraction in banking employment during 1968, the Negro proportion of the remaining work
force was greater than it had been before. How much this point
can be generalized to a highly competitive job market situation
such as would result from an economic recession is very difficult
to say. However, it should be noted that banks in general have
an extremely high turnover rate in the normal course of affairs
(largely attributable to the high proportion of young females on
the work forces) and have very horizontal employment structures
with short lines of upward movement in any given job position.
It is therefore reasonable to assume that in the event of a recession of moderate strength, the banking reaction would probably be more one of not hiring to augment the work force than
one of laying off existing employees. The effect on Negroes
would therefore more likely be one of a contraction of the employment opportunities of Negroes not yet hired. There is no
question that in a highly competitive labor market, Negro applicants, who at the moment tend to be more often marginal
applicants, could easily be passed over. There is also no question that a continuation of the tight labor market which now
exists in many city markets will work to the benefit of Negro
job applicants

GOVERNMENT PRESSURES

Government pressures take two general forms. The first is
through legislating whatever regulations and sanctions are
deemed necessary, to restrain discrimination or promote job opportunities, and the second is through the promulgation of attitudes which serve to set the level of expectations of industry
members as to the "seriousness" with which government views
the legislation it has enacted.

Acting either alone or in consort with various other forms of
social and broad economic pressures evidenced above, govern-

ment activities have almost always been a spur to increased Negro employment. The next sections evaluate the effects of both legislation and governmental attitudes on a local level in three specific job markets before returning to the national situation.

New York City Experience, 1945-1966

The legislation on minority employment rights traces its history to the "New York State Law Against Discrimination," which established what is now known as the New York State Division of Human Rights in 1945.[62] This law established the pattern for similar legislation in the majority of other states and undoubtedly influenced the form of the Civil Rights Act of 1964.

We have already seen from the national statistics that the progress of racial and ethnic minorities in banking was very slow from the end of World War II until the late 1950's. During this period, the New York Commission Against Discrimination (predecessor of the New York State Division of Human Rights) made a number of informal investigations into complaints concerning banks. At the end of August 1958, the Commission tabulated its activities in this area.[63] A study of that tabulation gives some insights into the speed of progress.

The complaints themselves are of relatively minor significance. There were fifty-two filed against banks or trust companies during the thirteen year period by forty-seven different persons, almost 90 percent of whom were clerical workers. Forty-nine of the fifty-two complaints were in New York City. Over 60 percent of them alleged discrimination because of color and the majority of complaints arose from dismissal from employment actions. Five of the cases remained open as of the end of August 1958, but of the twenty-nine complaints of color discrimination which were closed, "probable cause" was found in only three. These were "adjusted by conference and conciliation," in the words of the Commission. However, in a pattern often followed by compliance agencies, the Commission did not restrict

---

[62] *New York State, Law Against Discrimination* (1945), Art. 15, Executive Law, Ch. 118, Sec. 296.

[63] *The Banking Industry: Verified Complaints and Informal Investigations Handled by the New York State Commission Against Discrimination, July 1, 1945 - August 31, 1958*, (in the files of the Commission). (Mimeographed.)

itself to investigation of specific allegations, and in 55 percent of the cases some discriminatory practices or policies were disclosed and adjusted, whether or not they pertained to the specific complaints made.

As a result of the informal investigations, the Commission was often able to collect data on Negro employment and employment trends. The statistics, presented as Table 28, are spotty at best, and not meant to be precise. Total employment figures were reported as of some specific day during the year reported, and it was not the same day in each case. Often it was an approximate number. The number of Negroes reported was sometimes based on managerial estimate and sometimes on head count; confusion was occasionally evidenced between Negro and Puerto Rican job holders.

It is interesting to note the progression of Negro employment during this period when employment levels were not subject to federal pressures but were taking courses largely determined by the philosophies and policy determinations of individual bank officers under the spur of the state law. As might be expected under these circumstances, there is considerable variation in the results.

Overall in the eight examples cited, there were about five times as many Negroes employed in 1956-1957 as there were in 1949-1950, which indicates some progress even though employment in the base years was very low and the banks were growing rapidly. It is well to remember that the early 1950's were not characterized by social activism on the part of corporations, and as a result the progress made by Negro employees advancing in the firms was much more likely progress based purely on merit. If there was such a thing as a "traditional Negro job" evident at the beginning of this period, it was for male Negroes in the guard, messenger, and porter categories. There were still many Negroes in these jobs six years later; but additionally, there was the beginning of representation in a wide variety of clerical positions, an increasing number of public contact teller jobs, and even a (very) few managerial and official positions.

One of the banks was running what was obviously a "Jim Crow" operation, using its Negro employees almost exclusively in its black branches in Harlem and Washington Park. For the period, this probably did more good than harm, as the only black branch manager noted among the eight cases appeared in

TABLE 28. *Negro Employment, Various Banks* *
New York City, 1945-1958

Year	Employees		Notes
	Total	Negro	
			Bank A
1949	2,800	0	None had ever been employed.
1950		5	All girls hired for clerical positions.
			Reportedly, one Negro applicant had received serious consideration for a position as a cost accountant, but failed the physical examination.
1951	3,000	16	Clerks, typists, machine operators, trainee, messenger, and cleaning women.
1952		22	
1954	4,000	36	15 clerks, 8 machine operators, 5 typists, 3 messengers, 2 junior bookkeepers, 1 bookkeeper trainee, 1 stenographer, 1 matron.
1956	6,200	117	Including now two junior tellers and a junior teller-trainee.
			Bank B
1950	3,000	0	None had ever been employed.
1952		5	Two supply clerks, three female clerical workers.
1954		9	Seven clerical.
1955		12	Eight clerical
			Bank C
1950	2,500	75	All working in branch offices. All except one teller were armed messengers or porters; all males.
1951		76	One stenographer added. Five other Negroes had been hired in clerical positions, but had left.
1954		115	25 clerical workers, 90 messengers, etc.

TABLE 28 (Continued)

Year	Employees Total	Negro	Notes
			Bank D
1948	8,000 (including foreign)	3	All clerical positions.
1949		30	Includes teller trainee, registered teller, dividend clerk, clerk-typist, draftsman, librarian, plus twenty employed as cleaning women, porters, matrons, and elevator operators.
1950		37	Seven additional Negroes hired including 4 pages and 3 clerical workers.
1952	7,100	50	Approximate number.
1953		75	Estimated.
			Bank C and D
1955		200-250	Various clerical positions. No Negroes on staff strictly as janitor or porter.
1957	13,000	300	Includes an assistant head of files and a chief checker in documentary division.
			Bank E
1952	1,000	24	Fifteen as guards or in maintenance jobs.
1953	2,500	( )	Entire maintenance staff Negro. Additionally, there were 40 clerical workers.
			Bank F
1947	1,900	( )	Twenty-four clerical workers, 20 were at Harlem branch. Negro messengers used throughout system.
1948		( )	Thirty clerical workers. One head bookkeeper. Four other clerical promotions during the year.
1953		90	Some Negroes in each of 77 branches. Branches in Negro areas (Harlem and Washington Heights) very largely Negro, but managers and assistant managers white.

TABLE 28. (Continued)

Year	Employees Total	Negro	Notes
			F Branches of E and F Bank
1954		90	Includes one assistant manager.
1955			Promoted to manager. Also one head teller.
1956	1,450	100-120	Seventy-five guards and messengers.
			Bank G
1947		5	Two file clerks, 1 messenger, 1 junior clerk, 1 typist.
1949		20	
1950		30	
1951		41	
1953	8,000	105	Two tellers of 700 employed.
1954	9,500	122	
1955		171	Positions include assistant section head, teller, head bookkeeper and bookkeeper, senior and junior clerk, stenographer, typist, clerical machine operator, messenger, and guard.
1956	10,600	256	Includes also section head, elevator operator, telephone operator, and investigator.
			Bank H
1950	341	1	One real estate inspector. One Negro real estate appraiser had been employed but resigned to take position as executive vice president of a Negro savings and loan.
1951		4	One real estate inspector still employed, 3 typists.

Source: Condensed from: *The Banking Industry: Verified Complaints and Informal Investigations Handled by the New York State Commission Against Discrimination,* July 1, 1945.

*The Commission study gives names of the individual banks involved but there is no advantage to reporting them here. All save the last were among New York's ten largest.

Note: All figures are approximate.

this bank. Another bank was, with equal obviousness, trying to avoid establishing "traditional positions" for its black employees by assigning them to various jobs in the organization but employing none in janitorial or porter positions.

However, few sociologists or other investigators felt that the apparent advances made by Negro workers in gaining entry to the industry were sufficient. One unpublished 1957 study of attitudes and practices toward minority hiring and upgrading in suburban areas adjacent to New York City felt:

> The postwar attitude of management toward Negro workers in our limited sample does not appear to have undergone any drastic change. Business officials in the interviews we conducted speak more often than not in the same terms as those quoted [in 1946].
>
> *   *   *   *
>
> Circumstances have changed since World War II. Negroes have benefited, like nearly everyone else in the country, from the present economic boom . . . [but] . . . private industry still has far to go. Negroes are still frequently the last to be hired and the first to be fired. Furthermore, they are not being provided with the [right] kind of motivation.[64]

The authors of the above study reflect a position which seems pervasive to the point of universality among researchers into minority hiring by major firms in New York City or elsewhere: that "something is being done, finally, but it is not enough." This attitude is especially prevalent among compliance agencies.

A report prepared eleven years later by the Equal Employment Opportunity Commission for the Commission's hearings on discrimination in white collar employment in New York City, January 15-18, 1968 echoes the same sentiments:

> On the basis of the 1966 data, banks and insurance companies as a whole rate high in overall white collar employment of both [Negro and Puerto Rican] minorities, compared to major corporate employers in manufacturing and those in publishing, advertising and broadcasting. . . .

[64] Bernard Rosenberg and Penny Chapin, *Management and Minority Groups: A Study of Attitudes and Practices in Hiring and Upgrading* (unpublished: in the files of the Industrial Research Unit of the University of Pennsylvania, 1957), pp. 147-148.

Actually, only two or three [among the ten or fifteen largest firms] in each of the two industries had made significant progress in equal employment by 1966 and were continuing to make progress in 1967. Many of the larger firms were still doing poorly. Some of them still exclude Negroes and Puerto Ricans completely from managerial and professional jobs.[65]

This last paragraph might seem somewhat harsh in light of the fact that by 1966 the banking industry in New York, both in absolute numbers and relative to the size of its work force, employed more Negroes in white collar jobs than any other major industry in the city except hospitals. The Commission is absolutely correct in pointing out that many banks, and some very large ones among them, were not contributing to the Negro employment gains. Table 29, taken from the EEOC report verifies the wide disparity in Negro participation in nine dominant banking firms. Notice that the firms labeled "F," "H," and "I" had no Negro employees in technician, professional, or official and manager categories. (Firm "D," more than likely defines "technicians" somewhat differently than do the other firms, a problem which we have encountered before.)

The nine firms in Table 29 are very definitely dominant firms in the industry. Their total white collar employment of 52,173 is five times the aggregate of the forty-six smaller banks also included in the survey. Their average work force size is 5,797, compared to 235 for the smaller banks. Comparing the 7.1 percent Negro white collar participation in the large banks with the 4.4 percent rate of the smaller firms reflects the fact that large banks in general provide more than average proportional job opportunities to Negroes.

Between 1966 and 1967, the EEOC noted considerable change in the level of Negro utilization by the large banks.

The nine large commercial banks as a group made substantial gains in Negro employment in one year, their participation rate for Negro white collar workers rising from a collective 7.1 percent to 10.2. One bank moved from 9 percent

---

[65] Equal Employment Opportunity Commission, *White Collar Employment in the New York City Financial Community* (Summary of Report). (New York: The Commission, 1968), pp. 2-3.

TABLE 29. The Banking Industry
Percent Negro Employment In White Collar Occupational Groups
New York City
1966

Occupational Group	Total Number of Negroes	Total NYC Banking	46 smaller banks	Percent Negro										
				Total	Nine dominant banks									
					A	B	C	D	E	F	G	H	I
Officials and managers	77	0.7	N.A.	0.7	0.6	1.0	0.7	2.1	0.7	—	—	—	—	—
Professionals	35	1.1	N.A.	1.3	1.0	3.8	2.7	1.2	2.8	—	0.9	—	—	—
Technicians	57	5.2	N.A.	6.2	1.8	1.3	3.3	18.6	—	—	—	—	—	—
Office and clerical	4,638	8.2	N.A.	8.8	11.6	9.8	10.3	9.7	8.9	5.2	4.7	3.1	2.8
Total white collar	4,811*	6.7	4.4	7.1	9.0	8.3	8.0	7.9	7.1	4.5	3.8	2.7	2.2

Source: Equal Employment Opportunity Commission, White Collar Employment in the New York City Financial Community (Summary of Report). (New York: The Commission, 1968), Tables 4, 5, and Appendix E.

* There is a discrepancy of four persons in this column total which is not accounted for by EEOC.

to 13.4 percent and another from 7.9 to 12.8 percent. Even the bank with the lowest percentage increase rose by 1.1 points, from 4.5 to 5.6 percent.

Total white collar employment in this group jumped by 7,179, with an increase of 2,377 in the number of Negro white collar employees. . . . this suggests that one of every three hires was a Negro, a rate proportionately five times higher than that in the past.[66]

These are obviously tremendous gains in one year and the hiring rate reported for Negroes is extremely high. The Commission's report added an emphatic caveat:

However, these gains must not be misinterpreted. The vast majority of the new Negro employees (2,229 of the 2,377) were placed in office and clerical work.[67]

Actually, this is itself an optimistic note, for it indicates that in ten years the "traditional" jobs in banking in New York City had moved up from the porter-messenger-guard type positions to general clerical. And the 148 Negroes hired directly into the higher-level white collar positions represent about one-fifth of the total number of Negroes employed on all levels, both white collar and blue, which could be accounted for in seven major banks and one small one ten years previously.

Obviously, the EEOC is right to suggest that more could be done in providing job opportunities to Negroes in New York City. On the other hand, it is difficult to conceive of situations in which "more" could not be done. If banks throughout the country had equaled the experience of New York City during this period there would be little cause for concern.

The Baltimore Experience, 1959-1967

It took the Baltimore Community Relations Commission ten years to get the commercial banks of Baltimore to agree to provide quarterly statistical reports showing their involvement with Negro employment and their rates of Negro hiring. The Commission's Tenth Annual Report, for 1966, measures the progress which had occurred in banking in the preceding nine months:

---

[66] *Ibid.*, p. 14.

[67] *Ibid.*

Total employment of Negroes rose from 6.5% to 8.3% of the work force in the banks while "white collar" employment showed a similar rise from 5.5% to 7.0%. About one in five new employees during the first six months of 1966 was a Negro.[68]

In the first six months of 1966, 176 Negroes had found new white collar employment and 199 in all job classifications in Baltimore's seven commercial banks. The Commission recognized the gains: "These figures represent encouraging progress in the involvement of Negroes in the commercial banks of Baltimore." [69] The inevitable disclaimer follows: "The breakdown of the figures, showing in more detail where the increase and new hiring took place, is disappointing, however." [70]

The report then continues, to show that Baltimore's banks had no Negro officers, and that during the six months of new hiring, only two Negro administrative assistants and four Negro administrative trainees had been hired. Finally, it asks for higher banking wages (to cut down turnover during the early months of employment), and for more sophisticated recruiting methods and improvement in interpersonal relationships (to hold and attract qualified Negro employees).

A somewhat later report by the same Commission gives detailed information on Negro employment and hirings by Baltimore's commercial banks for 1966 and the first quarter of 1967.[71] These data are in Table 30, where it is seen that Negro white collar employment rose from 6.6 percent to 7.7 percent over the twelve months, and Negro overall employment from 7.9 to 9.0 percent. These numbers (which do not reconcile exactly with the Commission's previous, 1966 report) show a 24.7 and 19.7 percent growth in Negro white collar and general employment respectively (which the Commission would call a 1.1 percent rise in each case, were it to follow similar examples in its 1967 report). This is substantial growth, and reflects an aggregate hiring rate for the seven banks of 17 percent Negro

---

[68] Baltimore Community Relations Commission, *Tenth Annual Report, 1966* (Baltimore: The Commission, 1966), p. 20.

[69] *Ibid.*

[70] *Ibid.*

[71] Baltimore Community Relations Commission, *A Summary of the Employment of Negroes in Commercial Banks in the Baltimore Metropolitan Area* (Baltimore: The Commission, 1967).

TABLE 30. *The Banking Industry*
Employment by Race
Baltimore Metropolitan Area
1966-1967

For Quarter Ending	All Employees			White Collar		
	Total	Negro	Percent Negro	Total	Negro	Percent Negro
3/31/66	4,627	366	7.9	4,302	283	6.6
6/30/66	4,858	411	8.5	4,535	326	7.2
9/30/66	4,716	395	8.4	4,418	321	7.3
12/31/66	4,803	416	8.7	4,502	335	7.4
3/31/67	4,869	438	9.0	4,561	353	7.7

Source: Baltimore Community Relations Commission, *A Summary of the Employment of Negroes in Commercial Banks in the Baltimore Metropolitan Area* (Baltimore: The Commission, 1967), Table III.

over the period, at least a fair proportion of which must be attributed to the activities of the Commission. Nevertheless, the Commission is again quite right to point out the lack of Negro officers in Baltimore's banks and the relatively heavier representation by Negroes in the entry-level and low-paying jobs of lower-skill demands. Table 31 shows a representative quarter's job classification breakdown for Negro and non-Negro employees.

More than 25 percent of non-Negro employees in the Baltimore banks are seen to hold jobs in the two highest classifications, compared with slightly over 1 percent of Negroes. Machine operator, junior clerk, and various blue collar jobs account for seven out of ten Negro employees, compared with three out of ten non-Negro employees in these generally unglamorous jobs. (It is interesting to note that about as many of Negroes as whites are in teller jobs, despite the general sensitivity of that position.)

In addition to being low-paying, the jobs held most frequently by Negroes are also generally entry-level positions. One explanation for this occasionally offered by bankers but disclaimed by Negro interest groups is that Negro turnover is higher than for whites, which would tend to increase the proportion of Negroes in the entry-level jobs. The Commission's 1967 report contains

TABLE 31. *The Banking Industry*
Employment by Race and Occupational Classification
Baltimore Metropolitan Area
March 31, 1967

Occupational Classification	Employees				Percentage Distribution	
	Total	Non-Negro	Negro	Percent Negro	Non-Negro	Negro
Officers	585	585	—	—	13.2	—
Administrative assistants	558	553	5	0.9	12.5	1.1
Administrative trainees	69	67	2	2.9	1.5	0.5
Senior clerks	512	492	20	3.9	11.1	4.6
Machine operators	627	507	120	19.1	11.4	27.3
Tellers	924	840	84	9.1	19.0	19.2
Stenographers	268	267	1	0.4	6.0	0.2
Junior clerks	782	681	101	12.9	15.4	23.1
Clerk typists	224	206	18	8.0	4.7	4.1
Other trainees	12	10	2	16.7	0.2	0.5
Total white collar	4,561	4,208	353	7.7	95.0	80.6
Service employees	308	223	85	27.6	5.0	19.4
Total	4,869	4,431	438	9.0	100.0	100.0

Source: Baltimore Community Relations Commission, *A Summary of the
Employment of Negroes in Commercial Banks in the Baltimore
Metropolitan Area* (Baltimore: The Commission, 1967), Table I.

data not only on employment levels but also on hirings. There
do seem to be some statistical aberations in the Commission's
tables, and so our Table 32, which follows, should be used only
as possible indication of turnover differences rather than a precise measure, but it does seem to show that Negro turnover in
Baltimore in late 1966 and early 1967 was considerably higher.

What does all of this indicate about the status of Negroes in
banking in Baltimore? It is most instructive to look back a
few years in order to obtain some base data for comparison.
In the Third Annual Report of the Baltimore Community Relations Commission (under its previous title of "City of Baltimore

TABLE 32. *The Banking Industry*
Turnover Rates by Race
Baltimore Metropolitan Area
Fourth Quarter, 1966 and First Quarter, 1967

	Negro Employment		Non-Negro Employment	
	4th Quarter 1966	1st Quarter 1967	4th Quarter 1966	1st Quarter 1967
Employment at beginning of quarter	395	416	4,321	4,386
Employment at end of quarter	416	438	4,386	4,431
Net gain during quarter	21	22	65	45
Hired during quarter	65	88	325	448
Left during quarter	44	66	260	403
Quarterly turnover rate [a]	10.9	15.5	6.0	9.1
Indicated annual turnover rate	52.9		30.3	

Source: Baltimore Community Relations Commission, *A Summary of the Employment of Negroes in Commercial Banks in the Baltimore Metropolitan Area* (Baltimore: The Commission, 1967), Table I.

[a] Defined as number of employees who left during quarter divided by average employment during quarter.

Equal Employment Opportunity Commission"), we find that in 1959, seven years before the data shown above were collected, not only were there no Negro officers in the commercial banks of Baltimore, there were no Negro employees at all.[72] In October of that year, the Commission had been forced to postpone a conference of the City's commercial banks called to illustrate to them the positive experiences of a large New York City bank with Negro hiring because six of the larger banks invited refused to attend. It required threats of investigations and hearings by the Commission to obtain the attendance of all but two of the banks at a rescheduled conference but even then in the

---

[72] City of Baltimore Equal Employment Opportunity Commission, *Third Annual Report* (Baltimore: The Commission, 1959), p. 8.

Commission's words: "Those representatives who did attend were reluctant to discuss the issue." [73]

Between October 1959 and October 1966, not only had the open feelings of hostility toward integration on any level in banking been overcome, but one out of every twelve jobs in the industry had become Negro held, and about one person in eight or nine being hired was Negro.

Washington, D.C., December 1965

In December of 1965, the Commissioner's Council on Human Relations of the Government of the District of Columbia prepared a survey of employment in banks, savings and loan associations, and insurance companies.[74] Thirteen of the District's fifteen banks were included. (One "Negro bank" was not included, and one other bank refused to provide detailed data.) The Council found that among the 3,632 persons employed, 474, or 13 percent, were Negro, but that over half of the Negro employees were in the two lowest job categories, as "unskilled" or "maintenance" workers.

The Council's statistics provide both positive and negative inputs. On the positive side, proportionally more Negroes (13.0 percent of the work force) work in the District's banks than do in the banks of almost any other city, or than do in the savings and loan associations (7.2 percent Negro) or insurance companies (10.2 percent Negro) in the District. On the other hand, only two of the 474 Negroes held jobs as officers in these thirteen banks, and the Nation's Capital is the most heavily Negro populated major city in the country.

The Commissioner's Council noted:

> With the exception noted [a bank founded by an "interracial group"], all District banks employed Negroes in 10 percent or less of skilled positions. These proportions were constant, whether the banks were large or small, new or old, whether or not the bank had adopted a formal "equal employment" policy. . . . There is no correlation between formal, or informal, equal employment policies and the level

---

[73] *Ibid.*

[74] Government of the District of Columbia, Commissioner's Council on Human Relations, *Summary of Survey of Patterns of Discrimination in Banking, Savings and Loan Associations and Insurance Industries—Washington, D. C.* (Washington, The Council, 1966).

of equal employment achievement. . . . There are few indications that the banks are promoting these equal employment policies with any vigor.[75]

Whether the Council's overt pessimism is warranted, the survey does show very few Negroes in the highest job positions, and the report provides one of the best breakdowns available of job categories. With some rearrangement and the addition of the "percent of column totals" figures, the survey's results are reproduced as Table 33, where the wide disparity in job distributions among whites and nonwhites should be noted.

TABLE 33. *The Banking Industry*
Employment by Race and Occupational Classification
District of Columbia
December 1965

Occupational Classification	Employees				Percent Distribution	
	Total	White	Non-white	Percent non-white	White employees	Nonwhite employees
Executives						
President	12	12	—			
Exec. Vice Pres.	12	12	—			
Senior Vice Pres.	38	38	—			
Vice President	77	77	—			
Unspecified a	13	13	—			
Total	152	152	—	—	4.8	—
Junior Officers						
Asst. Vice Pres.	79	79	—			
Treasurer	3	3	—			
Asst. Treasurer	30	30	—			
Cashier	17	16	1			
Assistant Cashier	72	71	1			
Unspecified	80	80	—			
Total	281	279	2	0.7	8.8	0.4
Chief Clerks						
Chief Clerks	8	8	—			
Asst. Chief Clerks	33	31	2			
Total	43 b	41 b	2	5.0	1.3	0.4

---

[75] *Ibid.*, p. 2.

TABLE 33. (Continued)

Occupational Classification	Total	Employees		Percent non- white	Percent Distribution	
		White	Non- white		White employees	Nonwhite employees
Tellers						
Head Tellers	53	53	—			
Senior Tellers	108	106	2			
Tellers	431	387	44			
Unspecified	1	1	—			
Total	593	547	46	8.0 [b]	17.3	9.7
Clerical						
Secretaries	126	124	2			
Clerk-typists	153	143	10			
Clerks	807	753	54			
Machine operators	324	275	49			
Unspecified	839	774 [b]	63			
Total	2,249	2,071 [b]	178	8.0 [b]	65.6	37.5
Unskilled [c]	98	50	48	49.0	1.6	10.1
Maintenance	216	17	199	92.1	0.6	41.9
Total	3,632 [b]	3,157	474 [b]	13.0 [b]	100.0	100.0

Source: Government of the District of Columbia, Commissioner's Council on Human Relations, *Summary of Survey of Patterns of Discrimination in Banking, Savings and Loan Associations and Insurance Industries—Washington, D.C.* (Washington, by the Council, 1966), p. 12.

[a] Some institutions provided no breakdowns within the larger categories. Such figures were reported as "unspecified."

[b] *Sic*, minor arithmetical problems are indicated which we have not attempted to correct.

[c] Includes runners, guards, chauffeurs, messengers, and kitchen staff.

National Legislation and Compliance Attitudes

The examples taken from the individual cities, above, have two things in common. First is that under the spur of legislation and the active interests on the part of human relations commissions and other compliance groups, Negro employment levels showed a marked improvement. Second is that compliance organizations are almost invariably pessimistic about the results which have obtained, regardless of what those results reflect. The same is also true in dealing with national legislation and national compliance agencies.

Appendix C scans the legislative and regulatory history of activities by the federal government relating to equal employment opportunity (without detailing the content of the legislation). There it can be seen that in recent years, the number of agencies involved and the complexity of the legal requirements have grown immensely. So has the amount of time which bank managements in general devote to personnel activities, and personnel managers specifically devote to civil rights activities.[76]

Much of the thrust of the national compliance agencies' activities has been devoted to sensitizing top managements in banks to the problems of Negro employees. The more sophisticated compliance groups recognize that this is a much more important factor than any imposing of sanctions.[77] It is probable that this is the reason that most compliance agencies on all levels are extremely hesitant to issue a statement of unqualified optimism on any aspect of the banking employment situation; for the momentum of the advance of Negro employment will be lost if bank managers are allowed to become complacent about their activities to date.

Simultaneously, the sanctions available to the compliance groups have occasionally been applied. As of the end of 1968, four small southern banks had lost their federal deposits because of refusals to take action to meet the equal employment opportunity requirements. This action "has served notice to the entire banking industry that the Treasury Department will use sanctions for noncompliance when it is necessary."[78]

There can be no doubt that this strategy on the part of compliance groups—consisting of working from the top of firms down, of being perpetually dissatisfied with results so far re-

---

[76] The President and the Chairman of the Board of one of the country's largest banks report that they now spend two-thirds of their time on personnel problems. From: "Why Citibank is More than a Bank," *Business Week*, November 16, 1968, p. 83.

[77] Interview with an officer of a Federal compliance agency, September 1968.

[78] Robert A. Wallace, before the U.S. Commission on Civil Rights, San Antonio, Texas, December 13, 1968, quoted in "Federal Banks Increase Minority Employment Nearly One-Third in One Year," *Fair Employment Report*, December 23, 1968, p. 131.

corded, and of showing judicious amounts of regulatory muscle
—has had considerable effect on the level of Negro employment
in the banking industry. Very few bankers pretend that the
same results would have been obtained had the activities of the
federal, state, and local governments not been so visible. There
are, however, no firm indications whether increased legislation
will result in the Negro employment augmentations seen in the
largest of the city banks to spread to the numerous, smaller
establishments located throughout the country.

Effects of the Regulation on Smaller Banks

The effects of the regulations in influencing equal employment
policy formation have been seen primarily in the larger, city
banks. These banks seem to operate not in fear of the sanctions
which could be imposed against them (although these could be
severe) but rather in fear of the adverse publicity which would
accompany their imposition. The smaller banks are not so conscious of publicity. Additionally, they are shielded by their numbers from the federal compliance agencies. With over 13,000
commercial banks in the country, any individual, smaller bank
is invisible to compliance agencies unless in flagrant violation
of the regulations, or unless specific complaints call the bank to
the attention of these groups.

Although many smaller banks, particularly those in outlying
areas outside of the South, are unfamiliar with the details of
the federal regulations, most know that some form of sanctions
are possible in the event of noncompliance with equal opportunity provisions. Many of these smaller banks are believed to
feel that a dissatisfied Negro employee will be likely to file a
formal complaint with a government agency rather than use
internal methods for due process and grievance redress, thereby
bringing the firm to the government's attention.

Under these conditions there would be logic to a bank's being
particularly careful in screening Negro applicants in order to
avoid government notice, and the result would be fewer Negro
job opportunities in these banks. We have no evidence that this
pattern is pervasive among smaller firms in the banking industry, but do not doubt that were it so, increased legislation would
provide little remedy.

Overall, legislation and regulations have been effective in
sponsoring the beginnings of Negro employment, and the ac-

tivities of the compliance agencies have been effective in promoting sensitivities to this cause and in furthering employment gains. Considering, however, the already complex regulatory base (as seen in Appendix C) and considering that many firms have not yet understood or assimilated the existing regulations, there seems little need for additional regulation in this area unless they can be more effectively communicated to the smaller firms.

CHAPTER VII

Some Problems of Negro Employment

As is the case in most other industries, the employment of Negroes in banking has created some problems for managements with which they did not have to deal a few years ago. In this chapter, we shall examine the problem areas which are usually cited and which potentially have application to an industry as skill-structured as is the banking industry. The analysis will be concentrated in three general areas. First, we shall evaluate the impact of Negro hiring on white employees; second, we shall examine the severity of the problems with the behavior patterns which many Negroes bring to the workplace; and third, we shall investigate the possibility that there may be some incremental costs to employers who currently have larger numbers of Negroes in their work forces.

IMPACT ON WHITE EMPLOYEES

There are three areas of potential difficulty associated with the impact of increasing number of Negro employees on the whites who were there before them. First, there are the upsets which are sometimes associated with the initial employment of Negroes; secondly, there is the possibility that when any given department or section of an organization reaches a certain percentage Negro, whites will tend to no longer apply for jobs there; thirdly, there are situations which can arise from the integration of facilities such as water fountains or washrooms.

Reaction of White Employees

Before banks generally became integrated in their employment structures, the greatest fear on the part of managements was the reaction which might be felt from white customers of banks, but there was also some question, especially in the South, as to how employees would accept Negroes as co-workers. In an earlier chapter we found that the fear of bank managements as to the reaction of their customers was largely unfounded, and that even when Negroes began to be placed in sensitive, public contact jobs, customer reaction was minimal. In Table 14 (in Chapter IV) the reactions evidenced by customers were classified, and those reactions were found to be about evenly split between positive and negative.

The concern by most banks for the sensitivities of their employees was understandably less than that felt for their customers. A very few of the banks interviewed by the author indicated that concern in this area had been a major factor accounting for their lateness in beginning Negro hiring. The reaction of the employees reported by the forty-seven banks which were included in the survey bears out the fact that this was not a significant factor. These are categorized in Table 34.

TABLE 34. *The Banking Industry*
White Employee Reaction Reported to Influx of Negroes
47 Commercial Banks Surveyed
United States, 1968

Type of Reaction	Severity		
	None	Minor	Severe
Voluntary white terminations	40	7	0
Isolation of Negroes	43	4	0
Other expressed resentment	32	15	0
Favorable employee reaction	42	5	0

Source: Data in the author's possession.

In the cases involving voluntary terminations or early retirements noted among white employees, in Table 34, no more than two persons were known to be involved from any one bank. (Some banks, particularly in the Northeast felt that a few more employees may have terminated for this reason without indicating to management why it was that they were leaving.) In any event, we can see that there were very few examples of expressed dissatisfaction on the part of white employees and very little obsruction from them to their banks' providing employment opportunities to Negroes.

The probable cause for this overall lack of disruption, aside from the relatively high class of person which chooses a bank as a place to work, is the very deliberate way in which most banking establishments added Negroes to their work forces. The rate of growth of Negro employment in most banking firms has been slow enough to forestall any feeling of being threatened with job displacement on the part of whites already employed. (Also involved is the high turnover rate which banks have experienced over the past several years.)

All Negro Departments

Considering the short time that Negroes have been hired by the banking industry in any significant numbers, it is reasonable to anticipate higher concentrations of Negroes in entry-level jobs than elsewhere, and this of course exists. During interviews, however, it was found that very few banks reported any significant concentrations of Negroes in such areas as custodial and cafeteria services. Only one bank showed a custodial force that was entirely Negro. In other jobs, however, there were some significant concentrations. Twenty of the forty-five banks which responded to a question asking if Negroes were found in higher concentrations in some jobs than in others indicated higher than proportional numbers of Negroes in the proof and transit sections, with figures ranging as high as 30 percent of employment in those sections. Twelve of the banks, all of them located in eastern urban centers, reported high concentrations of Negroes on the night shift. One of those banks indicated that 60 percent of its night employees are Negro, and this bank and several others felt that the Negro proportion on the night shift was changing more rapidly than they thought desirable.

For banks which have night shift requirements in urban population centers, it is apparently becoming increasingly difficult to lure white employees, and specifically white female employees, to the center city areas for work at night—despite shift differentials and other benefits. Although it is obvious that none of the night shifts reported have become exclusively Negro, several large banks are anticipating the time when this will happen. A few others are also looking forward to the time when similar results may obtain in the proof and transit section, in data processing sections, and in other machine-oriented departments. Those banks which feel that this sort of *de facto* internal segregation might harbor potentially serious problems for the future, might be well advised to devote attention to seeing whether these jobs can be made more attractive to everyone or can be distributed throughout the organization rather than having them clustered in a single location.

Facility Integration

The integration of facilities, such as locker rooms, washrooms, and water fountains has occasioned serious difficulty in some industries.[79] There were, however, so few Negroes in the banking industry during the period when segregation was a general practice in this country that separate facilities were seldom constructed. Therefore, banks have inadvertently been spared any problems connected with their integration.

NEGRO BEHAVIOR PATTERN PROBLEMS

Although it is generally true that the behavior patterns which Negroes newly entering the job market bring with them to their place of work are also shared by the majority of whites of the same social class and background, it is also true that banks have been unfamiliar with both until recently. Generally speaking, the most qualified Negro applicants for jobs in banking as elsewhere were absorbed by those progressive employers who began hiring Negroes before they were really compelled to do so. When the combined compulsions of government activities and social pressures forced the balance of firms to begin hiring Negroes, those firms found that the number of Negroes required who could meet the entry-level skill demands could not be found. Therefore, many firms were forced to re-evaluate their entry standards, such as the requirement for a high school education, and other evidences of past achievement, in order to obtain a sufficient number of Negroes. These same standards then had to be applied to whites seeking entry-level employment. In a large number of cases, the result has been that bank managers must now contend with new employee behavior patterns, from both whites and blacks, from which their higher entry-level requirements had protected them in the past.[80] These new patterns show up in work efficiency, in attitudes, and in a few other areas.

---

[79] Herbert R. Northrup, *The Negro in the Rubber Tire Industry.* The Racial Policies of American Industry, Report No. 6 (Philadelphia: Industrial Research Unit, Wharton School of Finance and Commerce, University of Pennsylvania, 1969), pp. 117-119.

[80] Interview with Herbert R. Northrup, "On Hiring Hard-Core Jobless," *U.S. News and World Report*, October 14, 1968, p. 85.

Work Efficiency

It is very difficult to measure the actual output efficiency of employees without engaging in an extensive study program on this point alone. There are, however, certain manifestations of work behavior which are related to efficiency and about which many have felt concerned for some time with respect to Negroes. Absenteeism, tardiness, and mysterious disappearances from the place of work are among the areas most often mentioned as sources of difficulty. The response of forty-seven bankers interviewed on their experiences with Negro as compared with other employees in these three areas are classified below in Table 35. The table shows that a great majority of the banks interviewed found no differences between the races. It also shows, however, that no bank considers its Negro employees to be superior in regard to these work habits.

TABLE 35. *The Banking Industry*
Reported Work Habits of Negroes Compared with Non-Negroes
47 Commercial Banks Surveyed
United States, 1968

Response	Frequency
Reporting for Work on Time	
No difference seen between races	31[a]
Others better	10
Negroes better	0
No comment	6
Regularity of Attendance	
No difference seen between races	30[a]
Others better	11
Negroes better	0
No comment	6
Terminating Employment Without Giving Notice	
No difference seen between races	29
Others better (less frequently)	10
Negroes better (less frequently)	0
No comment	8

Source: Data in the author's possession.

[a] Includes four exclusions of "Hard-Core" employees in each case.

Also closely related to work habits is the question of turnover. Turnover among Negro employees in some industrial occupations has been characterized as "amazingly high." [81] This factor perhaps deserves special consideration in the banking industry, where our data indicate the average turnover rate of all employees for 1967-1968 in our survey banks was already something over 32 percent per year.

The forty-seven banks interviewed were asked whether their turnover rates had been analyzed and if they had any feelings about the primary composition of that turnover. Remarkably few of the banks had made any calculations or analyses of Negro turnover differentials. Only eleven commented on Negroes at all. Of those, three banks felt their Negro employees had turnover rates which were the same as for others in the work force; three other banks felt that the Negro turnover rate was somewhat more; and one felt it to be twice as high. Additionally, there were some more complex feelings. One bank stated that Negro female turnover was less than other female turnover, but that Negro male turnover was higher than other male. Finally, one bank said that although Negro turnover averaged out to about the same as for others, there was less "averageness" to the ratio; that bank felt the probability that a Negro employee would leave in the first week or two was very high, but that if this period was passed, the probability was also high that a Negro would stay permanently.

Only two banks had actually performed analyses of turnover by races. One of these found Negro turnover to be almost twice as high as for whites, and the other found it to be five percentage points higher. (They are both eastern, urban banks.) There are two structural factors which might be thought to influence the results seen: time on the job, and sex. Females, and especially young females, have higher turnover rates than do males. But since the male-female ratio among Negroes is about the same as it is among non-Negroes, this factor should not affect the turnover ratio. On the other hand, time on the job very definitely is a factor. Banks which had analyzed their turnover on a time basis found that 60-78 percent of their yearly turnover was made up by persons who were in their first year of employment. Because a much higher proportion of all Negroes working in banking establishments has been recently hired, we should

---

[81] *Ibid.,* p. 83.

expect the overall Negro turnover rate to be somewhat higher
as a result.

Communications Difficulties

We have already noted some of the difficulties which bankers
have experienced with their Negro applicants concerning poor
basic education, poor work history and skill development, and
bad speech habits and verbal skills. Except for some communications difficulties, these factors are not specific to Negroes, but
grow from a sociological experience of urban poverty—which has
been the lot of a proportionally larger number of Negroes than
whites. Thus, the consequences of this experience are more
often seen in banking employment among Negroes than among
whites. For bank managements, this has often meant that additional training has had to be undertaken at the workplace, and
training of a more basic sort than banks had previously had to
perform.

A problem more specific to Negroes is that of verbal usage and
general communications. One of the manifestations of this may
have been seen above in the somewhat larger proportion of Negroes reported to terminate their employment without giving
notice or telling the employer of their plans. To at least some
degree, the communication breakdown seen between the employee
and the management is a result of the employer not recognizing
the sociological gap between himself and a Negro employee, and
therefore presuming a communication pattern when none exists.

These difficulties are intensified when it comes to "hard-core"
or other culturally deprived employees. Two fairly typical
stories illustrate this communication problem. In Chicago, a
young, "hard-core" Negro employee repeatedly reported to work
unshaved. After several warnings by a supervisor, the case was
referred to the bank's personnel department, where careful ques-
tioning was required to find out that the youth had never used a
safety razor and was afraid of cutting himself with the straight
razor which he owned.[82]

A similar story comes from a West Coast bank which reported
that one Negro employee had come fairly close to being fired
when he offered as an excuse for not reporting for work the fact
that "his hog was stole." Only after the bank was able to ascer-

---

[82] "Chicago Banks Hiring 'Unemployables' as Part of Federal 'Jobs Now'
Project," *American Banker*, August 8, 1967.

tain that a "hog" in slum parlance is a Cadillac did the excuse make any sense.[83]

Attitudinal Problems

The attitudes which employees bring with them to the workplace are partially conditioned reflexes. The child of a father who felt well-disposed towards his workplace and respected his employer will be more likely to have similar feelings himself than the child of a father who did not. Upbringing, environment, and personal ambition all have a part to play in setting the attitudes of a new employee, and again it seems that in much of American industry, the problems connected with poor attitudes are most visible among the Negro employees.

In response to a statement by "an official at one big company" that a "fairly high percentage of Negroes as compared to whites are totally irresponsible in their attitudes toward the company, the public, and their jobs," and engaged in "an unhappy and disconcerting degree of theft" and similar activities, the director of a Negro activist organization replied that these attitudes and activities were "common everyday occurrences" in Negro society—because Negroes have been excluded from the mainstream of society.[84]

Fortunately, as was the case with other problems with Negroes in the banking industry, the attitudes of Negroes in the industry toward their jobs and/or their employer do not show the grave cause for concern occasionally reported in other industries. Thirty-nine of forty-seven banks of our survey answered a question asking for a comparison between the attitudes of Negroes and other employees. Nineteen of those responding felt Negroes held the same variety of attitudes as non-Negroes; thirteen felt that others were better, and seven felt that Negroes were better. Four comments were also received concerning polarization of attitudes among Negroes—that is, that the good attitudes were very good, and the bad were very bad.

A question related to the preceding one was asked about the self-confidence exhibited by employees on their jobs. Here, twenty-eight bankers responded, with half indicating they could

---

[83] Interview, July 1968.

[84] "Nation's Biggest Firms Now Committed to Help Solve the Racial Crisis," *Wall Street Journal*, June 11, 1968.

see no difference between the races, and only ten finding that perhaps their Negro employees did not yet feel fully at home.

These results can be interpreted to mean that the banking industry has attracted neither a large number of "Uncle Toms" nor a large number of "black power" types or other activists. We found similar results previously when we examined the propensity of Negro employees to join unions in banks. It is possible that Negro job seekers do some self attitudinal-prescreening before looking for work in an institution closely associated with the "establishment" such as a bank. The true activists, in other words, do not bother to apply. The same, undoubtedly, is true on the part of a number of the truly unprepared.

THE COSTS OF NEGRO EMPLOYMENT

The problems that we have covered so far, including lack of qualifications and preparations on the part of Negroes, attitudinal incompatibility, job demands, white employee or customer reaction, and discrimination on the part of bank managements are among the arguments most frequently raised to explain why more Negroes are not currently employed in the banking field. There are two other important factors which need to be investigated: One of these is the number of Negroes who apply for jobs in banks—a point which we shall discuss in the next chapter; the other, less frequently mentioned argument is that employing a Negro or other minority group member is more costly than employing a white.

We have seen that, by and large, the skill level, the credentials, and the work history which the banks see offered to them by entry-level Negro applicants is lower on the average than it is for whites. Additionally, many firms are exhorted to seek deliberately "underqualified," the "culturally disadvantaged," and the "hard-core" to provide them with not only the opportunity to work, but also the rehabilitational training and special handling necessary to bring them to a performance level acceptable to the firm and its customers. Most of these "culturally disadvantaged" are Negroes. It is reasonable to assume, therefore, that banks which have a large number of Negroes are undertaking more special training and a wider variety of training than are banks employing very few Negroes. It is also possible that the level of competence demonstrated on the job by these employees is somewhat more costly to banks which have a large number of Negroes.

On the other hand, if the additional training procedures which may be required for new Negro employees can be effected by existing staff through increased sensitivity, reorientation of techniques, or other devices requiring only the redirection of discretionary managerial time, if the training period is not so lengthy as to be overly costly to the firm, and if the results of the training are reflected in skill levels and behavior patterns accepable to the firm—then there is no reason why a pattern of employment which includes greater numbers of Negroes should be more costly. It is even possible that, because of training procedures, increased sensitivity, and special attention, post-training efficiency and behavior patterns might be better (less costly overall) than would have been the case had standard employment procedures been followed.

Statistical analysis on this point, comparing operating efficiencies among some twenty large banks having widely different proportions of Negro employees has led us to the conclusion that there is no cost-related variable associated with employing Negroes which is strong enough to affect earnings per employee. The coefficient of correlation between change in earnings per employee and change in Negro employment was calculated as —.000256.

SOME PERSPECTIVES OF PROBLEMS WITH NEGRO EMPLOYMENT [85]

It would be surprising indeed if the employment of Negroes in banking had not brought with it some problems which bank managers had not had to face before. Yet it seems clear that the banking industry has suffered less and has seen fewer difficulties and disruptions in integrating its work forces than have many industries. This is partially a result of the Negro applicants to the banking industry being better prepared and better attitudinally adjusted to the rigors of work force participation than many of their counterparts who apply to more industrial firms. With a few exceptions in the custodial sections of banks, the lowest of banking jobs is half-way up the industrial scale found in many other firms. As a result of this, Negro (like

---

[85] During the investigations and interviews to collect the data which has been presented in this study, some perspectives were gained into bankers' reactions to the problems stemming from Negro employment. These were felt to be of sufficient interest to be included here. They are opinions of the author and should be interpreted as such.

white) applicants to the industry apparently go through something of a process of self-screening; the worst do not apply.

Undoubtedly, all banks would prefer better qualifications, better past histories, more premotivation, and more evidenced ambition from Negroes. Some banks, and particularly the smaller ones which are relatively less experienced, continue to indicate they feel that having finally made the effort of offering opportunity to the disadvantaged, that they should be rewarded by gratitude and superior performance. They are looking for "dream Negroes" and they have seldom found them. Nevertheless, banking managements' experiences with Negroes have seldom been especially trying. Banks have been almost uniquely free of the incidents between employees which have marred the integration of some industrialized firms. They have been protected by the high level of sophistication of their existing work forces, by the characteristics of the bank work environment, and by the deliberate, careful way which most carried out the integration of their establishments. Banks broke no new ground in providing employment to Negroes; but although this retarded the entry of Negroes to the industry, it made the subsequent transition less painful.

Not only was the transition sociologically tranquil, it has also been economically unobtrusive. Undoubtedly, there are costs associated with the employment of Negroes which would not have been experienced had they not been hired. We can find no relationship, however, between a gross measure of the performance of banking firms and the relative level of Negro employment. Nevertheless, organizational changes have been required in both the structure and the behavior patterns within management.

Organizational Changes

The organizational structure of most banking firms has had to be modified within the past few years to reconcile them to the fact that among Negro applicants (and increasingly for all applicants) the level of skill development and motivations which individuals bring to the job are in need of remedial attention. Especially among the urban banks, where this is a particular problem, firms in the industry have had to take up remedial education to supplement the appalling level of learning which is the unhappy output of today's city school system. To banks, this means training in reading, writing, and arithmetic as well as in specific requirements related to banking's needs. This has already required considerable redirection of managerial activities in banks, and more will be needed in the future. (Banks have every right to expect better levels of performance from the output of the city school systems, and might be well advised to consider pressures in this direction as an excellent avenue for social involvement.)

Another area in which banks face new problems is with attitudes seen among Negro employees—toward work itself as well as the work place. Many bankers new to dealing with Negro employees undoubtedly have difficulty in sorting out how they, themselves, should react. Extremely few bankers are openly racist; on the other hand, extremely few bankers are experienced enough with Negroes to be "openly open." Most are bombarded by conflicting statements and personal experiences and often do not know how to react. As an example, consider the story of the stolen "hog" earlier in this chapter. Any bank personnel manager is sufficiently at home with the expected behavior and speech patterns of a white employee that, being informed of the stolen "hog" he would automatically question the employee further to find out what really did happen. But in reacting to a Negro making the same statement, many bank managers would hesitate.

Closely alligned with this problem is one of communications verbiage. Some bankers have attempted to ape the patois of the slum, but the sounds made are not only silly, they are also transparently insincere. For example, one eastern bank (not included in the survey) has issued a recruiting piece titled "Break Into the Bank, Baby," which appears in comic book form. This may be a sensitive recognition of the different social values of the slum, but one suspects that those to whom it has appeal might find more compatible employment in another field. Even in the interests of promoting the sociological benefits of increased Negro employment, there is little reason for bankers to compete with parking lot operators for sources of employees.

In training, discipline, and other necessary on-the-job communications, many bankers have shown a propensity to cover their confusion as to what constitutes a proper reaction toward Negroes by formalizing the personnel structure. Many bankers apparently feel more comfortable in dealing with Negro employees if they have some rule or standardized procedure, such as an internal regulation to fall back on. For example, rather than face the individual sensitivities of new Negro employees on some matter such as proper dress on the job, a bank might instead institute a formalized procedure, such as an internal "charm school" in which proper dress, speech, and poise are taught. Such devices, of course, must extend to all equally, regardless of race.

As a result, many personnel activities in banks are becoming more structured and more bureaucratic. To the degree that this has brought about a more orderly personnel activity in banking by replacing unnecessary traditions and limiting the whimsicalities of autocratic control, it has benefitted the industry. Insofar as it has substituted unnecessary bureaucratic procedures, it is dysfunctional.

Nevertheless, it is probably true that having to contend with the sensitivities of Negroes in their work forces has generally had the beneficial effect of requiring personnel departments to be more careful, more diverse, more imaginative, more attuned to the needs of the work force, and generally more sophisticated. This is an unexpected and seldom mentioned positive outgrowth of Negro employment.

How far personnel departments have come in this is the subject of the next chapter.

CHAPTER VIII

Banking Activities in Support of Increased Negro Participation

Despite the problems, and sometimes to overcome them, bank managers have undertaken a large number of activities in support of increased Negro participation. These activities have spanned the entire range of the personnel function. Additionally, many banks have also become involved in other projects closely related to the urban Negro crisis which, although not concerning employment directly, are part of the new social involvement pattern of banks.

AFFIRMATIVE ACTION

"Affirmative action" is: "positive or firm or aggressive action as opposed to negative or infirm or passive action." [86] It has been interpreted by an undersecretary of the Treasury as follows:

> *"Affirmative action"* means applying management techniques and controls over personnel actions that are normally applied to any program that you want to succeed. It means analyzing the methods, procedures and results of personnel actions to determine whether they have resulted in the exclusion of qualified or trainable workers because of race. It also means taking direct and appropriate corrective action if discrepancies are found between policy and practice.[87]

There is no consensus among bankers as to what the requirement for affirmative action actually calls for. As part of the interview in the banks sampled, two questions were asked concerning affirmative action: (1) How does the bank interpret "affirmative action?" (2) Do you feel that this carries the connotation of "discimination in reverse?"

---

[86] Section 301 (1), Exec. Order 10295, 26 Fed. Reg. 1977 (1961).

[87] Robert A. Wallace, before an Equal Employment Opportunity Workshop (New York: September 26, 1967), in "Equal Employment Opportunities," *Proceedings of the Workshop on Equal Employment Opportunities sponsored by the American Bankers Association* (New York: American Bankers Association and American Jewish Committee, 1967), p. 6.

All forty-seven banks were asked the first question, and there were, essentially, forty-seven different answers. Most of the responses reflected specific (although often vague) activity goals, such as "encouraging Negro applicants," or "insuring the company from top to bottom is attuned to equal employment opportunities," or "taking any action beyond what you would normally take to gain Negro employment," or "establishing liaison with minority group members who are willing to do some preselection for us," or even "doing what is right." Several bankers felt affirmative action meant "doing exactly what we are doing now." Only three banks, two southern and one midwestern, felt it meant "equal treatment regardless of race." (It is interesting to note that the personnel policies and practices manual of that midwestern bank contains no reference to equal employment opportunity.)

The question on whether affirmative action carried with it connotations of "reverse discrimination" was not asked in all cases. But among twenty-two responses collected, fourteen bankers felt it did, only seven felt it did not, and one bank felt that "preferential recruitment but not preferential hiring" was implied.

Whatever "affirmative action" does actually mean, it is fortunate that many bankers are better at practicing it than vocalizing it. Most of the larger banks throughout the country, although they may interpret "affirmative action" in different ways, have instituted programs aimed at increased minority utilization. A typical program was outlined in a letter from a major, southern bank to the Chairman of the Equal Employment Opportunity Commission in response to a question from the Commission in early 1968. It contained seven major points, summarized below.

(1) Our company has established an equal employment opportunity policy which has been communicated throughout the bank among both officials and employees, and to the community through employment advertising.

(2) We recruit administrative and management trainee candidates at most of the major Negro colleges and universities in the state. We also visit all of the predominantly Negro high schools in the area in recruiting clerical employees.

(3) We have established contacts and sound working relationships with several influential members of the minority communities and have outlined our equal employment op-

portunity policy and enlisted their support in referring applicants.

(4) We have worked very closely with almost all of the governmentally supported programs aimed at preparing minority groups for more meaningful employment. We have also worked closely with the Urban League and State Department of Labor to obtain qualified applicants.

(5) We have carefully reviewed our battery of tests in order to determine absolute minimums for the particular tests that are relevant to given jobs. We have also experimented with pictorial and non-verbal tests in an attempt to minimize the effect of heredity and environment.

(6) Our interviewers have been encouraged to utilize their interviewing skills in determining applicants who seem to possess maturity, initiative, and sound judgment but who might not measure up to our minimum requirements on all of our clerical tests. A number of these applicants have been hired for entry level positions which would utilize their strongest qualifications.

(7) We have encouraged supervisors to promote their minority employees from entry level jobs to more responsible positions in order to provide positions for which marginally qualified applicants might be considered.[88]

We shall look more specifically at several of the areas which are raised here, such as recruiting, testing, and training later in this chapter. Many banks do have affirmative action programs covering areas similar to those noted above and reflecting change from older personnel practices in varying degrees.[89] (Some of these are included in the next chapter.) Before we examine the more specific aspects of these programs, however, we shall have to acknowledge that in practice many equal employment opportunity programs are constructed more for the purpose of public relations than for the purpose of setting personnel procedures. The Plans for Progress program, consisting primarily of a public

---

[88] Letter in the author's possession.

[89] A nice summary of a bank's affirmative action program in the public domain is that by Mr. David Rockefeller, President, The Chase Manhattan Bank, before the Federal Equal Employment Opportunity Commission, New York, January 16, 1968. We would do it injustice by summarizing it here, but the full text is available from the Public Relations Department of The Chase Manhattan Bank.

posture of affirmative action in minority employment on the part
of many of the nation's largest firms, has come under fire for
this very point. In analyzing the statistics for firms which were
and were not members of the program in New York City in
1966, the Equal Employment Opportunity Commission found that
minority utilization in the "Plans for Progress" firms was "substantially lower" than for companies not party to a comparable
public pledge. [90] This has led to some question as to the continuing utility of that program, especially now that minority representation reports (another aspect of the Plans for Progress
program) are required of all banks with over twenty-five employees.

In a similar vein, one large California bank supplied the
author with a copy of a special edition of the company's news-
letter magazine as evidence of the distribution to employees of
information concerning the bank's stance on equal employment.
In the magazine's lead article, entitled "Equal Employment Opportunity in Practice," pictures are included of fourteen orientals,
nine Negroes, two persons who are possibly Spanish-Surnamed
Americans, and twenty-three others. In the balance of the magazine, other stories of general interest to the bank's personnel are
included. In these stories, photographs containing recognizable
pictures of 292 persons are included. Among the 292, exactly
three are Negro: one of these appears as the subject of a picture
in a photo contest, and the other two are seen serving punch at
a branch opening. We have no doubt that this is unintentional,
but it does provide what may be a sad insight into the sincerity
of the lead article.

Another example comes from an interview in a southern bank
in which a personnel manager spoke at great length and in
glowing terms of the effectiveness of a Negro preinduction training center in providing well-qualified Negro entry-level employees
for his organization. Unfortunately, a check in the records revealed that over a two year period, only one employee in the
bank had come from that organization.

Many bank organizations devote more effort than perhaps they
should to telling the government and interviewers what they feel
the interviewers want to hear. There is no question that bank
participation in many of these areas is overstated. But there is

---

[90] "EEOC Looks Into New York City Employment Patterns, Finds Minorities Substantially Under-Represented in White Collar Jobs," *White Collar
Report* (No. 567), January 18, 1968, p. B-3.

no evidence that a "conspiracy of hyperbole" exists among bank managers, and it is only reasonable to allow for some aggrandizement through self-recognition and self-praise; often this is the only specific recognition that bank personnel managers have received for their efforts in this field during the last two or three years. And even discounting this factor, the evidence is very clear that at least among many of the nation's larger banks, changes in personnel activities reflecting a new awareness of minority groups have come at an increasing rate and with increasing sensitivity.

In a remarkable number of cases in banking, this new sensitivity seems to flow from the top of the organization. In only two cases among the banks interviewed did the author find indications that the personnel manager had actually a higher degree of commitment to Negro employment than the bank's president to the point where the personnel manager felt he was undertaking new programs at his own risk. In part, this is a result of very good communication of equal employment needs and requirements to at least the larger banks which are in a position to hire a large number of Negroes. Both the Department of the Treasury and the American Bankers Association have figured strongly in this by arranging workshops and devoting conferences to these activities. A new, high-level committee within the American Bankers Association, the Bankers Committee on Urban Affairs, has recently been formed to evaluate existing programs and formulate new ones for involving the banking industry in not only providing jobs and job training, but also in other areas of social responsibility such as housing and business assistance.[91]

Part of any affirmative action program requires spreading the sensitivities developed among the officers of a corporation to the level of first line supervision. This is often portrayed as an extremely difficult procedure, but although it is clear that a positive stance must be taken with many first line supervisors, the approach need not be harsh. An excellent example of the handling of this situation is provided in the next chapter. Here let us examine some of the specific programs in recruiting, selecting, and training employees which have been undertaken by banks.

---

[91] American Bankers Association, *A Program for Urban Progress* (Washington: American Bankers Association, Bankers Committee on Urban Affairs, 1968), p. 2.

RECRUITING

Using turnover data and other sources, it is estimated that the forty-seven survey banks interviewed 458,800 persons in order to hire 70,417 during 1967. This indicates that in the average bank, 6.5 persons were interviewed in order to fill one job. The weighted average selection ratio is somewhat smaller than the simple average, indicating that smaller banks have been somewhat more selective than larger ones.

The nearly half-a-million applicants recruited by the industry were contacted through all of the usual recruiting techniques. Depending upon the traditions in individual cities and on the condition of the specific labor market, walk-ins, referrals, employment agencies, classified ads, and direct high school and college recruiting are all used. None of these sources is predominant in the industry for applicants. Walk-ins are the most common source in many cities, but where tight labor markets prevail, employment agencies are often mentioned. Referrals are often a major source of applicants as well.

Banks have undertaken special activities in connection with all of the employee sources in order to promote a larger flow of Negro applicants. The number of Negro drop-ins can be stimulated only by banks' indicating a general attitude of acceptance through other recruiting sources, and through the general expression of an equal employment policy in practice. The Department of the Treasury's Compliance Section has frequently exhibited a fear that Negroes were not applying to banks for employment. But although this may have been true as recently as two or three years ago, the author's spot check of banking hiring offices revealed that there is no longer great need for concern on this point. Thirty to fifty percent of persons seen there were Negro.

Special efforts involving classified advertising are somewhat difficult to evaluate. All banks which use classified ads indicated that they have requested the EEO tag lines as required by law, but since these tag lines appear in all classified advertising, they can provide no informational input to Negroes seeking employment, and therefore can have little effect. About one-half of the firms interviewed indicated that they had at some time or another placed ads in predominantly Negro papers, either of an institutional nature or actually seeking applicants. One bank mentioned that it knew of one employee acquired because of this form of advertising, but most bankers felt that such advertising was of token significance either for finding new employees or for aiding the image of the bank.

A few years ago, there were a number of private employment agencies specializing in minority group members, but these firms generally catered to blue collar and service occupations and few banks used their services. Some of these firms continue to exist, but on higher levels their functions have been generally taken over by the profusion of quasi-public Negro self-help organizations and firms engaged in "vestibule" training.

In the deep South, bank association with these groups, while growing, is still relatively limited. The surplus supply of qualified Negroes in the South is only now being absorbed to the point where banks have to seek "substandard" Negroes and install special training programs. In other areas of the country, banking involvement with these groups is heavy. One New York City bank alone reports that it cooperates with more than fifty antipoverty agencies, public and private, as well as five agencies serving the handicapped. Most of these are providing special sources of minority group recruitment. There are forty-two such programs in the city of Cleveland, alone, although the Cleveland banks do not deal with all of them.

Banks are involved with organizations or programs bearing such acronyms as PACT, TAP, CAMP, STEP, JOIN, WEB, AIM, MIND, CEC, WCEPT, CEP, BEEP, and others. Opportunities Industrialization Centers (OIC) have proved to be rather popular among bankers in cities where they exist, especially in Philadelphia. Dissatisfaction with this program was noted in only two cases. About half of the bankers interviewed mentioned the Urban League and the National Association for the Advancement of Colored People specifically, but six bankers felt dissatisfaction with the ability of local chapters of the Urban League to send referrals to the banks. The general feeling seems to be that although the Urban League's referrals are of a high quality and have definite skills and educational backgrounds to offer, there are not many referrals offered.

By far, the most popular of all of the special programs is that of the National Alliance of Businessmen, a program for providing employment for the hard-core jobless and summer jobs for disadvantaged youths. The NAB program was only about six months old when most of the banks interviewed were seen, and there was still some confusion as to the details of the program. But by that time, approximately 1,862 jobs for either the hard-core or for summertime employment had been pledged, and a fair number of them filled. Bankers' reaction to the employees hired under this program seemed optimistic, and although two banks reported bad initial experiences, most felt the program was working well, with about the normal drop-out rate. Few of the jobs filled had to be especially created.

Although few banks have had any luck with using local Negro businessmen or ministers as a referral source, four banks had obtained a few applicants in this way. One final example will perhaps make obvious that at least not all banking involvement with these special programs exists simply for its public relations aspects. One of the major New York City banks, for its own use, tallied the number of employees hired as a result of special-program minority group recruiting. It found that over approximately one year's time, more than 950 persons had been hired from these programs (including 400 young people hired for summer work). Although not all of this employment was drawn from predominantly Negro groups, the involvement is nonetheless extensive.

The type and degree of college recruiting performed by banks varies with the size of the organization. Many banks recruit throughout their states, and a few of the biggest cover major universities throughout the country. In the South, banks generally recruit at the Negro colleges to some degree, but they report the competition for the highly skilled to be intensive—not only from other industries, but also from the larger California, Chicago, and New York banks. Generally, banks have reported little success with acquiring Negro managerial candidates from the colleges. Many, however, have found that local junior colleges are often an excellent source of clerical employees. Especially in the South, many of the more ambitious Negro girls will apparently enter junior college with the expectation of staying only for a year or so, reasoning that this puts them at a competitive advantage for good clerical jobs. Both they and their schools are anxious that they be employed as rapidly as possible since job seeking rather than graduation is the primary goal. This has been found to be a source of prized employees at many banks.

Recruiting at high schools is almost always missionary recruiting, consisting of talks at career days, tours, occasionally sponsoring summer programs, and often trying to attract the attention of high school counsellors to steer qualifed applicants to the bank establishments. Very little direct recruiting is or can be done. New programs in this area which look promising concern potential high school drop-outs who are being given the opportunity to work part time and go to school part time until they complete their studies. Banks involved with these programs almost always report them to be among their best and most rewarding. We shall discuss some of them subsequently.

The final, major recruiting source for bank employees is other employees. Referral systems, whether or not they include a "bounty" are often the most important source of applicants. We have already noted that there has been some dissatisfaction with referral systems from EEOC because it was felt they tended to perpetuate the existing, low-minority racial mix in banks. Some banks, too, have indicated that they have avoided referral systems for fear of increasing the general dissatisfaction of the work force because of the number of friends of employees who might have to be turned down.[92] Four of our surveyed banks said that they were trying to overcome the first of these difficulties by making a special communications effort to Negro employees to refer in friends. Concerning the second point, although some referred applicants are inevitably turned down, banks which employ this recruiting system extensively report few difficulties with it. The selection ratio among employee referrals—that is the number of applicants who have to be seen in order to fill one job—is about three or four to one compared with seven or eight to one among walk-ins.

In the interview survey, bankers were asked for estimates of the racial ratio of their job applicants. Except in Phoenix, where Negroes are not the largest minority group, the minimum estimate was that 20 percent of those seeking work were Negroes. In New York and Philadelphia, the average was over 50 percent, and ranged as high as 85 percent for walk-ins. In the light of these figures, it is fairly obvious that Negroes do apply for jobs in banking, especially where they know that other Negroes are employed.

SELECTION

Standard procedure employed by banks in selecting new clerical-level employees consists of a screening interview, followed by a battery of tests, followed by interviews in greater depth. The

---

[92] This reaction has received judicial sanction in at least one case involving a textile mill. *Shirley Lea et al.* v. *Cone Mills Corporation*, U.S.D.C., Mid. Dist., N.C., July 29, 1969.

final selection of persons for employment is usually made by the personnel office, but occasionally by individual departments. Traditionally, banks have required a high school diploma for all full-time jobs. This requirement is now becoming a rarity in the industy. Almost all banks require employment and personal references, make credit checks, police checks, and occasionally other investigations as well.

It is currently in vogue to speak of the selection process as one of "screening-in rather than screening-out" applicants, but it is the inevitable nature of any selection process to screen out when the number of applicants exceeds the number of positions open. Most banks have interpreted "screening-in" to mean that they should examine their entry-level requirements very carefully to make sure that they are at the lowest possible level compatible with the position being filed. And in point of fact, since the entire training of personnel managers is to avoid filling jobs on a "first come first served" basis but rather to secure the best qualified employees at the least cost, most bank personnel managers continue to choose the best qualified, regardless of where the minimum standard level may be. Most will now, however, under a *ceteris paribus* condition give preference to a Negro applicant. For managerial positions, many report that a Negro applicant will be accepted over a white if the Negro's qualifications are 80 percent as good.

Overall, very little in the way of visible creativity can occur in the selection process itself. Most banks have relaxed their standards to some degree since 1965. Only three of our sample banks revealed that they continued, in 1968, to require a high school diploma for all jobs within their organizations; twelve others continued to require the diploma for all except special-program entrants (such as NAB or OIC); and five banks give preference to applicants holding a diploma. The remainder have dropped the requirement, generally without noticeable ill effects. The type of work offered by the banking establishments, and their general reputation, have insured that 90 and 95 percent of those currently applying to the industry come equipped with the high school diploma.

Testing

The tests normally used by banks for clerical-level applicants consist of mental ability tests (such as the Wonderlic Personnel

Test, the Otis Self-Administering Test of Mental Ability, or the Science Research Associates' SRA Verbal Form), tests of clerical abilities (such as the Minnesota Clerical Test, the Hay Number Perception Test, the Psychological Corporation's General Clerical Test, or the Short Employment Tests—developed by the Psychological Corporation specifically for the banking industry), and various proficiency tests for special skills (typing tests, stenography tests, language usage tests, office machine tests, and proof machine work samples). A number of other, less widely known tests are also used by individual banks.

All employers have been affected by recent regulations concerning the use of tests from the Equal Employment Opportunity Commission, various state human relations commissions, and the Secretary of Labor.[93] All of these agencies are fearful that employment tests, and especially mental ability tests, either contain inherent cultural biases, or may be being used by employers to unfairly exclude Negro applicants. The Secretary of Labor's order, which initially covered federal contractors employing 2,500 or more persons, contractors employing 1,000 or more beginning in September 1969, and all other contractors beginning in February 1970, is especially far-reaching. Essentially, it requires that all employers covered by the order who use tests to judge qualifications for hire, transfer, or promotion maintain statistical evidence that the tests are valid for the purpose used, and contain no inherent racial bias.

Although purporting to cover the validation of employment tests, this order actually contains verbiage suggesting a new definition of "unfair discrimination" and seems to cover all selection techniques. A portion of the order is reproduced below:

> Selection techniques other than tests may also be improperly used so as to have the effect of discriminating against minority groups. Such techniques include, but are not restricted to, unscored interviews, unscored application forms, and records of educational and work history. *Where there are data suggesting that such unfair discrimination exists*

---

[93] " 'Guidelines on Employment Testing Procedures' Adopted by Equal Employment Opportunity Commission," *White Collar Report* (No. 496), September 8, 1966, pp. C-1 to C-3.

Pennsylvania Human Relations Commission, *Affirmative Action Guidelines for Employment Testing* (Harrisburg, Pennsylvania: The Commission, 1967).

Willard Wirtz, *Validation of Employment Tests by Contractors and Subcontractors Subject to the Provisions of Executing Order 11246*, a memorandum to the Heads of All Federal Contracting Agencies, September 9, 1968.

(e.g., differential rates of rejecting applicants from different ethnic groups or disproportionate representation of some ethnic groups in employment in certain classes of jobs), then the contractor may be called upon to present evidence concerning the validity of his unscored procedures as well as of any tests which may be used. . . . If the contractor is unable or unwilling to perform such validation studies, he has the option of adjusting employment procedures so as to eliminate the conditions suggestive of unfair discrimination.[94] (Emphasis added.)

It is difficult to draw from the definition of "unfair discrimination" implied above any connotation other than that any selection procedure which does not provide hiring ratios in proportion of population percentages is unfairly discriminatory. A literal interpretation of this passage would require the implementation of quota systems which both Title VII of the Civil Rights Act of 1964 and Executive Order 11246 are very careful to avoid.

This most recent order of the Secretary of Labor was not yet in effect when our interview survey of the industry was conducted, and so no reaction to it could be collected. Subsequent conversations between the author and several bank personnel managers did reveal that some banks may be considering abandoning tests entirely as a selection device, but using them subsequent to hiring as a gauge of additional training which may be necessary, and to locate persons better in their initial job assignments. Several bankers expressed the hope that the American Bankers Association might coordinate validification studies for a number of banking jobs, which studies would apparently be acceptable under the Secretary of Labor's order.[95] This would not be an easy task for the American Bankers Association, or anyone else, for there are also some problems with how to validate a test for minorities. George K. Bennett, President of the Psychological Corporation, in commenting on the 1966 EEOC requirements for validating tests for minorities asked: "What is meant by this? Empirical validation? Content validation? How much generalization? Is it intended that if a test is equally valid

---

[94] Willard Wirtz, *op. cit.*, pp. 8-9.

[95] The American Bankers Association compiled information and made recommendations on test usage in 1952 in: American Bankers Association, *Clerical Testing in Banks* (New York: American Bankers Association, Customer and Personnel Relations Department, 1952).

for both groups but that the disadvantaged score lower a cor-
rection factor should be used? Such factor would be an indication of reverse discrimination and, moreover, would have to be
used on a judgmental basis since cultural deprivation is not all-
or-none but a matter of degree."[96]

Many feel that "critics of testing are not advocating test re-
form, but rather test abolition."[97] Banks will not be able to tell
whether this is the case until they see the method and degree of
enforcement of the existing regulations.

TRAINING

The special requirements of bank jobs, and the high degree of
efficiency and precision needed throughout the clerical levels but
especially in the teller functions, have meant that banks have
always been involved with special training programs. Stenography, typing, filing, and similar skills of a more general application have long been offered by secretarial schools, and are op-
tions in most of the public school systems in the country. High
schools and secretarial schools, however, do not offer teller
training.

In recent years, the larger banks have found it necessary to
supplement the special training programs required for their special job positions by more extensive teaching of basic skill development and refresher courses on the clerical levels, and many
have instituted courses on the managerial level and executive
level to sensitize top management personnel not only to technological and business advances but also to human relations problems and techniques. The training offered by one of the larger,
midwestern banks now consists of eight different courses in general orientation to the bank, its operations, and its customer relations policies; six courses in communications, dealing with telephone training, effective speaking, letter-writing, etc., and six
courses for secretarial training including typing and stenographic
skills. Additionally, clerical training is effectuated with the help
of nine courses ranging from the fundamentals of typing to
advanced keypunch training; supervisory and management

---

[96] George K. Bennett, "Ability Testing and the Culturally Disadvantaged,"
a document from The Psychological Corporation marked "Draft—10/6/66."

[97] Thomas E. O'Reilly, "Equal Employment Opportunity: A Mandate for
Today" (unpublished thesis, the Stonier Graduate School of Banking Conducted by the American Bankers Association at Rutgers—The State University, 1967), p. 64.

courses span the range from first line supervisor to officer level
and consist of twenty-three courses ranging from basics through
creative thinking, problem-solving, conference leadership, and
productive selling, to clever management techniques and officer
development seminars stressing behavioral sciences. Finally, four
courses are offered for in-house off-duty formal education.

This range of programs typifies the approach of the larger
banks, but does not reflect the changes occasioned in training
structures by the industry's involvement with the special needs
of minority group members. A more imaginative approach is
being formulated by one of the major competitors of the bank
whose program is outlined above. That program is being set up
with a "quasi-university" approach—that is, an offering of courses
is provided (twenty-five courses initially, but expanding) for
which employees may sign up as desired. The courses are run
on a semester basis, taking up to two hours per day—all on company time, with full wages. The courses fall into four basic
areas: (1) A "socialization" course for disadvantaged entrants
consists of remedial training, instructions in personal finance,
hygiene, work force participation requirements, and other "vestibule training." (This course is on a more concentrated time
scale, and takes place outside of the bank, but with full salary
during the training period.) (2) Education courses are offered
in vocabulary, arithmetic, and other areas. (3) Skill development courses are offered, not only for such things as teller position requirements, but also—for the girls—in charm, poise, etc.
(4) Management development courses dealing in finance, behavioral sciences, etc. are also given. This training is supple-
mented by a career counseling program designed to aid clerical-
level personnel in preparing themselves for promotion.

It should be no surprise that smaller banks do not have training programs as extensive as these. Most banks of all sizes have
some relationships with the American Bankers Associations'
American Institute of Banking, which provides courses and instructions in many cities.

In addition to the in-house training and skill development programs, banks engage in two other types of training programs:
special training for the "hard-core," and special programs with
high schools.

"Hard-Core" Programs

Through local chapters of the American Institute of Banking,
special training programs for the "hard-core" unemployed are

currently being conducted in New York City, Boston, and Wichita among others. The New York program involves thirty-four local banking institutions which have entered into a consortium arrangement to hire and train more than 700 "disadvantaged ghetto residents" for banking careers over a twelve-month period. The six week program involves thirty-two hours of classroom work each week, with teaching and counseling provided by the New York City Board of Fundamental Education, and on Friday afternoon of each week, the trainees—all of whom are hired prior to beginning training—return to their employing institutions where they report to a "buddy" who helps them make the transition into the work place. This six-week program is followed by an additional forty-six week period during which participants spend twenty-six hours of the work week on the job and the remaining nine hours in further classroom training. (This program has extensive federal funding.)

A similar program in Boston involves a group of seven banks, cooperating with the Opportunities Industrialization Center there, to train about sixty-five disadvantaged persons for achievement of proficiency in office skills. (This program also has funding through the United States Department of Labor.)

In Wichita, fourteen banks, in cooperation with the Urban League, structured and privately funded a seven-week skill training program conducted at a local vocational school. The program was designed to provide the trainees with a banking orientation. Remedial training was not involved, and trainees were not paid for classroom work.[98]

Two other very extensive programs in New York City have been established by banks which are not part of the AIB consortium there. Perhaps the most ambitious project is one sponsored by the First National City Bank under contract with the Department of Labor. This is an eighteen-month project which began in the Fall of 1968 and has as its goal the training of 700 persons for proficiency in clerical skills, language, and mathematics. All of the trainees are full-time employees of the bank, and during their sixteen to twenty-six weeks of off-the-job training, earn $65.00 per week. On graduation, they are automatically continued in employment by the bank, and all receive a ten-dollar raise. The bank expects its own financial involvement to be more than $150,000 for administrative and other services not covered

---

[98] A summary of the New York City program can be found in: "34 New York Financial Units, AIB, Join to Train, Employ Ghetto Youth," *American Banker*, July 8, 1968.

by the contract with the government. About 200 persons were covered by the program as of September 1968.[99]

The Chase Manhattan Bank also undertook an extensive special training program involving full-time off-the-job training in December of 1967. That program, called "Job Opportunities in Business" was undertaken without federal funding. It is one of the few such training programs in the banking industry which is oriented toward male trainees. Trainees are accepted in groups of about twenty, and the program consists of three phases. The first phase lasts six weeks, and includes forty hours of classroom training each week in oral and written communications, literature, basic economics, arithmetic, and orientation to the business world. Trainees receive $1.60 per hour pay during this time. During the second phase, trainees begin working, receive regular full-time salaries, and continue their remedial education on bank time. This phase may last for up to one year, and includes up to two hours per day of remedial education. The third phase is a follow-up phase of no specific time duration, and provides on-the-job coaching, individual development, and up-dating of educational achievements for any trainees who appear to need additional remedial education for specific positions. Other staff members may participate in this phase of the program on a voluntary basis.[100] This program has not been inexpensive, for the bank estimates that it has made an investment of more than $1,000 per student involved.[101] However, it has provided three significant benefits: it has achieved some sociological good by providing broader job horizons to trainees than they otherwise would have had; it has provided the bank with some well-trained new employees; and it has given the bank wide publicity at what would be modest cost for an advertising campaign of equivalent

---

[99] "Wirtz Visits Bank's School for Unemployed," *New York Times*, September 12, 1968, p. 71.

[100] The Chase Manhattan Bank, N.A. *Job Opportunities in Business Program* (New York: By the Bank, 1968). See also *Wall Street Journal*, December 23, 1969.

[101] "Training The 'Hard-Core'—A Top Banker Tells His Story," *U.S. News and World Report*, August 12, 1968, p. 51; the cost per employee estimate may somewhat understate actual costs. An officer of the New England Merchants Bank reported to the author in conversation that the "hard core" training program in which his organizaion participates (the AIB program mentioned earlier in the chapter) has a cost of $202,000 over a two year period. During the first year, twenty-six trainees were put through the program of whom twenty finished. This works out to a cost per trainee of approximately $5,000.

coverage. The program has been covered in *Newsweek*, and *U.S. News & World Report*, by the *American Banker*, *The New York Times*, *The Christian Science Monitor*, the Chicago, Illinois *News*, *The New York Post*, the Miami, Florida *Herald*, and even such papers as the Wooster, Ohio *Record*. Television and radio time in New York City has also been devoted to the project.

There has been more activity of this sort in New York City than anywhere else in the country. (There is also, of course, more banking and more Negro banking employment in New York City than anywhere else in the country.) Programs are also under way in Philadelphia, through the Opportunities Industrialization Center, in Los Angeles, through the Los Angeles City Board of Education, and in other cities. One of the most interesting of the new training programs is not supplied to the disadvantaged, but rather consists of making available the special training facilities of the larger, commercial banks to the membership of the (Negro) National Bankers Association. Through the American Bankers Association, and with financial aid from a government grant, twenty-two Negro trainees were placed, one each with an ABA member bank, for an intensive, year-long course of experience at the department head level. After the year of exposure to decision making in a large commercial bank, the trainee is expected to return to a black-owned NBA bank in a managerial position. (Management inexperience has long plagued the twenty-two Negro-controlled banking institutions now in existence. See Appendix "B.") The commercial banks sponsoring trainees pay them $7,000 to $9,000 during their year with them, and are responsible for seeing that the training offered can be applied to the black community.[102] This project is still in its formative stages.

Relationships to Schools

Many banks throughout the country, and with greater ranges of size than those which engage in the special programs noted above, have established special relationships with their local school systems whereby students in danger of dropping out are given the opportunity to work part time for pay in the bank. Very few adverse comments have been heard from bankers using this sort of a program, in that the programs not only pro-

---

[102] "White & Negro Bank Associations Launch Joint Project for Training Black Bankers," *Fair Employment Report*, April 28, 1969, p. 53.

vide sociological good, but also are an excellent source of pre-motivated, full-time employees. Very little specific classroom training is required, and the students actually perform productive work during their training. Thus, costs are relatively light, and the program can be engaged in by banks of almost any size.

The best documented, and perhaps largest, program of this type is sponsored by the First Pennsylvania Bank in Philadelphia. Several other banks in Philadelphia, as well as five area high schools, participate in the program.[103] Other company-sponsored training programs which involve on-the-job training for high school students are taking place in banks throughout the country. Often, these programs, too, provide not only sociological benefits for the bank, but also good public relations within the community.

OTHER BANKING ACTIVITIES

We have mentioned several times previously our conviction that the banking industry will be asked to expand its social responsibilities, especially in the area of urban affairs. In the past few years, individual banks, or local groups of banks, have provided financial support, either directly or through intermediary social organizations, to urban low-cost housing development, and to the development of black entrepreneurship and black businesses. The extent of this support has been significant. A quick scan of a few newspaper clippings, all from 1968, revealed the following: Philadelphia banks agreed to make up to $5 million in credit available to the city's low-income housing and rehabilitation program;[104] a group of Philadelphia banks announced a $2 million loan fund primarily to help Negroes establish new businesses in their neighborhoods;[105] a fifteen member bank group in Chicago had agreed to provide $100 million for interim financing of low-cost housing;[106] a San Francisco bank announced plans to advance

---

[103] For information on this well-documented program, contact the Personnel Department, The First Pennsylvania Banking and Trust Company, Philadelphia, Pennsylvania.

[104] "Banks Pledge $5 Million in Housing Aid," *Evening Bulletin* (Philadelphia), February 26, 1968.

[105] "Philadelphia Banks Join Agency, Form Loan Fund for Negro Ghetto Firms," *Wall Street Journal*, April 2, 1968.

[106] "Bank Group to Finance Low-Income Housing Plan," *Wall Street Journal*, April 5, 1968.

up to $100 million in real estate loans in minority areas throughout California; [107] eighty financial institutions advanced $100 million for homes in the Bedford-Stuyvesant section of Brooklyn; [108] a group of Philadelphia mutual savings banks provided a pool of $20 million for real estate mortgage loans.[109]

Evidence of an additional $68 million pledged by banks in New York City, Philadelphia, Houston, and Boston is found in Appendix "B." All told, these individual and group efforts—and probably there are many others not included here—have made available very close to $400 million in special loans or loan funds for low-cost housing and Negro business financing. Although this is a considerable sum of money, the fact that it is provided by individual banks or groups of local banks has deprived the industry of the additional publicity benefits which would have been derived through a more concerted effort. Everyone is familiar with the insurance industry's famous billion-dollar pledge, but relatively few realize the existence and significance of the banking industry's activities in these fields. (Undoubtedly, one of the functions of the American Bankers Association's Bankers Committee on Urban Affairs will be to insure that future activities of the banking industry in this area are well-directed, and do not go unnoticed.)

SUMMARY

Overall, it appears that, although the banking industry's involvement with locating, employing, and training Negroes for the industry commenced slowly, it is now moving very rapidly, especially among the larger banks. Even though they seem to have difficulty defining precisely what it means, bankers do seem to be undertaking affirmative action in opening up job opportunities, and in recruiting and training Negroes and other disadvantaged persons. At the same time, bankers have been expanding their social responsibilities to include increased attention to urban problems. There are some exceptions among the smaller banks, but these activities have been almost exclusively within the purview of the handful of largest banks in the country, and even among them there are banks not participating in the changes taking place within the industry.

---

[107] "California Banks Join Drive to Aid Easier Ghetto Loans," *New Pittsburgh Courier*, July 20, 1968.

[108] *Ibid.*

[109] "Mutual Banks Aid Philly Homebuyers," *New Pittsburgh Courier*, October 12, 1968.

CHAPTER IX

Policy Statements

In order to find out the extent to which equal employment opportunity has been formalized into policy statements, the personnel policy manuals were collected from four of the survey banks, one from each of the census regions. They reveal some interesting differences which reflect the divergence of reactions we have seen previously in the banking industry.

EQUAL EMPLOYMENT POLICY STATEMENTS

The manual obtained from the southern bank contains the strongest policy statement. It was given prominent display on the first page of the "employment practices" section of the personnel manual in late 1968, and reads as follows:

> It is the policy of this Bank to adhere to the requirements of Title VII of the Civil Rights Act of 1964, the Age Discrimination Law of 1968, and to all other legislation having to do with equal employment opportunities. We do not practice any form of discrimination, both in compliance with the law and as a matter of principle. We have long since informed our sources of manpower supply, and our management personnel, of our position of nondiscrimination in recruitment, training, and promotion.

> As part of the Bank's continuing affirmative action in being an equal opportunity employer, [name supplied] has been designated as the Bank's Equal Employment Officer. He will assure compliance throughout the Bank and with all equal employment laws and regulations; he will see that Bank personnel are assigned and utilized both for the Bank's best interests and so as to achieve maximum individual development and opportunity, regardless of race, color, religion, national origin, sex, or age; he will represent the Bank at conferences and other meetings related to equal

employment; and he will be available to discuss with any employee the Bank's equal opportunity practices.

Although this is a rather positive statement of an equal employment policy, it appears from its verbiage to have been influenced as much by a desire to satisfy the requests of the compliance agencies as to inform employees or request their participation in affirmative action. Other policy statements and personnel procedures in the same section of the manual do not dwell on past activities of the department.

Partially, this omnibus statement may have been included in reaction to the short-sighted views which characterized many compliance reviews conducted by federal agencies before they became more experienced. At that time, there appared to be something of an inclination on the part of those conducting reviews to be overly interested in not only written policy statements on equality of opportunity, but also in documentation that the bank had or would inform manpower suppliers, advertising agencies, and others of the policies of the bank, and would appoint in writing a high-ranking officer of the corporation as the equal employment opportunities officer.

The personnel policies manual of one of the largest of the eastern banks does not contain as directed a statement. The first section of the manual deals with "employee advancement and compensation," and contains the following statement:

> In considering candidates for advancement, the supervisor is required to make an objective selection based on merit. Included in this judgment are the individual's past performance, education, and work experience, as well as his aptitudes, interests, and attitudes. The choice of one member of the staff over another should be based on length of service only if both candidates are equally qualified in these fundamental respects. Race, color, creed, national origin, age, or sex are never to be impediments to advancement.

Another reference to the equal employment activities of the bank can be found in the manual, under "changes in employee status: placement." This is an extremely strong statement:

> The bank will not tolerate discrimination based upon race, color, creed, national origin, age or sex; disregard of this Bank policy will lead to disciplinary action. New employees

are selected upon their qualifications . . . and the requirements of the job for which they are being considered.

The policy manual of a smaller, western bank also contains
more than one reference to equal employment considerations.
Under "personnel aims," one of the ten aims mentioned is: "To
respect individual rights and to insure fair, courteous and con-
siderate treatment without regard to race, creed, color, national
origin, sex or age."

Making up the first page of the "policy statements," which
follow, another equal employment statement appears:

> It is our policy to select the best person available for each
> job opening. Hiring is based on ability to perform a specific
> job and on potential for growth and advancement. Race,
> color, religion, sex, age, or national origin will not be con-
> siderations.

Finally examined was the personnel policies manual of one of
the major north central banks. It contains no mention in its
102 pages of equal employment or race. (Worse, it contains one
passage on working conditions—smoking during working hours
—which seems to discriminate against females.)

This last experience—of not containing a policy statement in
the personnel department policy manual—seems to be a common
situation in the banking industry, even among the large banks
interviewed. Only eleven of the forty-seven banks surveyed said
that a statement appeared in their policy manual, although all
except four indicated that some method of distributing a policy
of equal employment opportunity had been undertaken at one
time or another. Fifteen banks had statements in employee
handbooks (or a separate statement given to all new employees);
seventeen had given space to these policies in the bank's house
organ (although there were indications in the last chapter that,
unless carefully handled, such statements can do more harm
than good); and in eighteen cases a letter from the president,
chairman, or some other official had been sent to all employees
at one time or another.

But it remains difficult to understand why so many banks,
even those which are apparently practicing affirmative action in
employment are so hesitant to include a statement to that effect
in the policy manual, or to make a continuing effort to insure
that all employees are kept aware of the policy. A suggested
draft of a policy statement prepared by the Department of the

Treasury for distribution at workshop meetings and, on request, to other banks, does not suggest that extensive verbiage is necessary for policy statements. The Treasury suggested draft is reproduced below:

> It is the policy of this (Bank) to implement affirmatively equal opportunity to all qualified employees and applicants for employment without regard to race, creed, color, sex, or national origin and positive action shall be taken to ensure the fulfillment of this policy. This obligation includes:
>
> > Hiring, placement, upgrading, transfer or demotion
> > Recruitment, advertising, or solicitation for employment
> > Treatment during employment
> > Rates of pay or other forms of compensation
> > Selection for training
> > Layoff or termination
>
> This policy of the (Name of bank) is consistent with the requirements and objectives set forth by the Presidential Executive Order 11246.
>
> The objective of the (Bank) is to obtain individuals qualified and/or trainable for the position by virtue of job related standards of education, training, experience and personal qualifications.
>
> Responsibility for ensuring compliance and continued implementation of (Bank)'s policy on equal employment opportunity is assigned to the (Officer and title).
>
> The responsible on site official and the (Bank) will review this policy every twelve months and measure progress against these stated objectives.

Despite the obvious grammatical and syntactical difficulties with this suggested draft, the elision from "policy" to "obligation," the lack of mention of age discrimination, and the reference to the Executive Order rather than the Civil Rights Act, there appears to be no reason why a statement of this sort should not be included in the personnel manuals of all banks.

AFFIRMATIVE ACTION STATEMENTS

One of the difficulties in disseminating an affirmative action pattern throughout an organization which is often voiced by bank personnel managers is the inability to communicate such policies with first-line supervisors. An excellent example of the spreading of such policies is included in the text of a speech presented by the personnel director of a major, southern bank to his personnel supervisors in June 1968. It covers the special problems of the disadvantaged, and then goes on to specify policy adjustments which the bank will require of first-line supervisors.

In presenting the policy changes to his supervisors, the personnel manager emphasized that reasonable policy adjustments in the method of selecting people would be made until such time as the minority group member should be able to compete more successfully on a merit basis. He also emphasized a willingness to provide extra time and training to allow Negroes to meet the high standards of his organization. The procedural policy changes themselves seem to make up an extremely well-balanced and sensitive program, and are presented in their entirety, below:

1. *Aggressively recruit* a certain percentage of "higher risk" people who with make-up orientation and skill training will have success on the job. The personnel department interviewer is the most skilled person to seek out and recommend the deserving applicants to you. Set priority jobs for Negroes. Some may be absorbed into existing easy-to-learn jobs. Where possible, jobs may have to be restructured to allow the person to grow into the position. Opportunities may be available to employ a person on a trial basis such as summer employment or maternity leave replacement. Entry level jobs may have to be redefined to the extent that they cannot be used for staffing higher level positions.

2. *Accentuate the positive* and use human potential with some innovation. In interviewing an applicant, instead of looking for what is wrong with the applicant, we need to look for what is right. Test results are not the sole determining factor. A person may score low because he is a slow reader but possesses other qualities which will permit success on the job. Carefully review the aptitudes and potentialities present in all forms of the personal interview.

3. *Broaden orientation program* jointly with the personnel department to include pre-work counseling—without which regular skill training often fails. Subjects should range from grooming, money management, transportation, babysitting, job expectations, work rules, cooperation, application

to duty, adaptability, communications, merit salary, benefits, company objectives, job titles, grievance procedure, to the more complex attitudes towards job, themselves, and community. Create a learning situation in which the trainee feels identified with the bank and its growth.

4. *Coach during training,* giving extra support to the learning process. Motivating the person to learn the total job and to expand beyond is almost as important as the actual training. Assign a work "sponsor" (the buddy system) for close personal training. Support techniques do cause a higher initial training cost but result in a more dependable worker over the long run. Make-up training as distinguished from normal training is necessary to bring a person up to standard in time available. Simple brochures available from manufacturers on "do's" and "don'ts" of the job are helpful.

5. *Frequent follow-up* is particularly important to monitor the progress or lack of progress of the individual. Because of deficiencies in background, careful supervision and more frequent appraisal is a must. Need for bank services and other needs should be recognized early and appropriate referral made with close contact continued until satisfactory solution.

It is difficult to imagine a finer statement of an affirmative section procedure; moreover, this statement was produced for internal use by the bank, and not for publicity.

CHAPTER X.

Determinants of Industrial Policy

Throughout this study, we have devoted our attention to cataloging the responses of managements in the banking industry, under varying conditions, to the economic, regulatory, and social pressures which have been associated with Negro employment advances over the past decade. In this concluding chapter, we shall assimilate that information in order to gain insight into the policy formulation patterns specific to the banking industry which those responses have produced.

In following the statistical presentations of the chapters, one factor which is readily apparent is that the banking industry delayed longer than most the inclusion of Negroes in its work force and the provision of meaningful job opportunities to members of that race. A second factor, equally apparent, is that once the banking industry did begin to act, it did so with reasonable vigor—at least on the clerical levels. From the 1940-1960 average of approximately 1.75 percent, Negro employment levels began to increase at a compound rate of about 15 percent per year. By 1968, the level had reached about 5.95 percent, and our current statistics on the rate at which Negroes are being added to the industry show that about one person in five now being hired is Negro.

A third factor which is also characteristic of the new employment patterns in banking is that the gains in Negro employment have been overwhelmingly on the clerical levels. Even our most recent statistics show that there are very few technical, sales, professional, managerial, and official positions held by Negroes. Finally, we have seen that there is considerable internal divergence within the industry in the Negro employment levels found.

We shall examine each of these factors in turn, and also discuss briefly the degree of social involvement now becoming apparent among banking managements.

162

INITIAL RESPONSE

Although the banking industry was among the last in the country to adopt an equal employment policy and provide meaningful job opportunities for Negroes, it is not apparent from our studies that overt discrimination was a major cause of this. Almost every aspect of the specific job requirements of the banking industry is unfavorable to the employment of Negroes, and additionally, there are several unique characteristics of the industry —especially those concerning its image—which have been important in holding back the initial entry of Negroes into meaningful jobs.

Job Characteristics

The lack of any significant number of blue collar job openings in banking has meant that the normal entry level requires a fairly high degree of skill development. Additionally, the skills demanded by the overwhelming majority of those entry jobs are such as can be performed equally well by either males or females. As a result, during the labor-short World War II years, the industry turned as a source of a new labor supply to females rather than to Negroes. Unlike many other major industries, banking arrived on the verge of the 1960's without any previous substantial experience with Negro employees.

One of the factors to which bank managers themselves call attention as having been important in delaying the acceptance of Negroes into the main body of the banking work force was a fear on their part of the potential reaction from employees and—more importantly—from customers. There is no way of knowing the degree to which this claim reflects an honest fear rather than an over-reaction on the part of banking managers or a methodology by which they transfer blame for inaction to other personnel within their organizations. But it is true that because of the structure of the banking industry and the sameness of the services rendered by individual banks a more violent customer reaction could have been a real possibility.

Image

Probably the most important reason for the continued inaction of banks in regards to Negro employment was the fact that the industry was under very low compulsion to become involved. The economic and work force considerations important to the industry were generally such that despite a rapid expansion in employment between 1945 and 1960 there were few pressures on the banks to seek sources of supply of entry labor alternative to the "safe" white, female, high school output. Sociological considerations were such during this period that very few Negroes bothered to apply to the banking industry. Also during this time, Negro advancement organizations were concentrating on industries which seemed to offer much greater potential gains. As a result, the banking industry was left very largely to its own devices and the image-conscious traditions of the industry seemed to have held sway, retarding the Negro employment progress.

Depositors in banks have always been interested in the security of their funds, and therefore in the security of their banks. Much of the decision making of the banking industry has therefore been traditionally aimed at presenting to depositors and to the general public an image of safety and conservatism—not only in the handling of monies, but also in the conduct of all banking operations. As a result, banks have usually been very slow to espouse new causes—whether in industrial, technological, financial, sociological, or organizational areas. Banks have seldom been the agents of change, and have usually shown an inclination to let others lead and bear the high initial risks of innovation. It is not unlikely that this same "wait and see" logic was applied by the banking industry to Negro employment. Without any compelling reason to hire Negroes, the banking industry felt no necessity to be on the forefront of sociological change.

ACCELERATING ACCEPTANCE ON CLERICAL LEVELS

Prior to 1960, a few banks, predominantly in New York City, experimented cautiously with customer and employee reactions to Negroes on the work force in other than custodial, guard, or service positions, and an occasional bank probed business relations by placing a few Negroes in jobs where they would be dealing primarily with other Negroes. But these experiments probably were not as important to the acceptance of Negroes throughout the banking industry as was the increasing acceptance of Negroes in industries elsewhere.

Lack of Artificial Barriers

It must have become apparent to the banking industry in about 1960 or 1961 that, although there was no overwhelming necessity to hire Negroes, there was also no longer any compelling reason *not* to hire them. Only then did the banking industry hiring patterns begin to change; but once changes began they spread through the industry with relative rapidity.

Part of the reason for this pattern, too, lies in the nature of the standard entry-level job in banking. In many other industries, artificial barriers had been erected through the years to protect the economic position of unskilled whites against erosion from inroads made by the expanding job horizons of Negroes no longer content with menial or agricultural work. There is convincing evidence that many of the segregation laws of the deep South were economic rather than sociological in their origins, and had the aim of making it more expensive to hire Negroes. However, once these laws were in effect, the barriers which they formed were interpreted as sociological and could only be battered down by concerted effort.

Within the banking industry, on the other hand, the barriers to Negro employment were very largely ones arising from the nature of the work itself. There was little need to erect elaborate devices to keep Negroes out of the industry, because under the prevailing educational and sociological patterns, very few Negroes could or would consider the industry in any event. This, coupled with the fact that the industry's attitude toward Negroes had been generally one of inaction rather than antagonism, meant that once affirmative action was undertaken it could proceed smoothly. As hiring did begin, bankers soon found that the fears which they had felt about possible disruptions attributable to white employee and white customer reaction were largely groundless allowing methodologies for including Negroes in the industry to be worked out easily.

The Negro population did not change so significantly from the 1950's to the 1960's that Negroes became significantly more attractive to banking managers. But several other factors were in effect in the 1960's encouraging bank managements to become more involved. In addition to the fact that it soon became a characteristic of the decade to expect special efforts from all employers to hire Negroes, one of the most important spurs to changing the attitudes of management was the increasing and continued pressure from government regulations and the threat of the possible loss of government deposits.

Additionally, the job market and economic conditions of the 1960's were considerably different than they had been during the 1950's. Profits were good, and most firms, including banks, were expanding rapidly. Personal mobility was increasing, so that banks were under pressure to seek out new personnel—not only to meet expansion needs but also to replace turnover losses. Simultaneously, the job market became exceptionally "tight," especially in keypunch and other jobs related to the new automation technologies. Banks, and especially the trend-setting urban banks, had to seek new sources of employees; and Negroes seeking industrial entry or job advancement were readily available. Together these factors encouraged new attitudes on the part of banking managers which, when tested by experience, produced the new hiring patterns which we have seen.

Drawbacks

With the current rates of hiring Negroes at approximately 20 percent on average for all banks, almost 30 percent for the major banks included in our survey of the industry, and well over 40 percent in certain of the major firms in New York City and Chicago, the banking industry is now adding Negroes to its work force faster than is the case in most other industries. There have been, however, two continuing drawbacks in the banking industry.

Being late entrants to the job markets for Negro clerical-level personnel, banks everywhere outside of the South found that the fairly small pool of well qualified Negroes had largely evaporated before they began to probe it. As a result, the experience of some banks in hiring Negro employees may have been that they found confirmation of the stereotype of ill-preparation, lack of motivation, and incompetence that many had anticipated. Fortunately, because these stereotypes had been feared, in many cases bank managements were prepared to combat them with affirmative action, and therefore were not unwilling to experiment internally with special training programs, buddy systems, and other special personnel procedures. These activities eased the transition to more heavily Negro work forces, and also seem to have had the beneficial side effect of producing a more organized, more sophisticated personnel function in these firms.

A second continuing drawback, often voiced by bank managements, has been the lack of an acceptable methodology for communicating the affirmative action stance of the firm to first-line supervision. Fortunately, here too there is evidence that practices are being worked out to communicate these ideas to supervisors and to insist on performance without being either fatuous or brutal.

CONTINUED LACK OF ACTION ON MANAGERIAL LEVELS

Despite escalating activities in increasing the numbers of Negroes on the clerical levels of banking organizations, there are still very few Negroes in higher positions in commercial banks. Partially this is because the supply of qualified applicants is limited. In discussing the effects of the job image perceptions of the banking industry on potential Negro applicants to it, we noted that there is very little reason for Negro college graduates to be premotivated toward, or attracted to, the banking industry. Additionally, banks which do extensive college recruiting have all noted the fierce competition among industries for the top quality Negro college graduates. Finally, the supply of "instant Negroes" who can walk directly into middle management banking jobs is limited and subject to the same competition.

Caution

It appears most probable that the lack of advancement of Negroes to managerial ranks in banking is at least partially attributable—in addition to the above factors—to the same "wait and see" attitude exhibited by bankers in beginning Negro employment at all. Advances in banks are always cautious, and there remains a flavor of experimentation with hiring Negroes for the higher-level jobs. Many bankers are not yet fully convinced that Negroes on managerial levels will be first, employees of the bank—and incidently, Negroes—or whether they will be first Negroes—and incidently, employees of the bank. As a result many of the officer-level jobs which are going to Negroes in the banking industry currently are in personnel or in public relations functions where the primary duties often consist of dealing with racial questions.

It is clear from the thrust of the recent governmental concerns that banks will be under increasing pressure to include greater numbers of Negroes at higher levels in their organizations. It was also apparent to the author that banks have not worked out the methodology for employing Negroes at high levels effectively. Three of the five Negro bank executives who were interviewed by the author volunteered (they were not asked) information indicating dissatisfaction with their current jobs, salaries, acceptance by their organizations, or advancement potentials.

INTERNAL DIVERGENCE

The more than 13,000 commercial banks of the country are joined together by an extensive network of correspondent relationships, by clearing house associations, by the Federal Reserve System, and by bankers associations on several levels. However, these are most often business relationships not involved with the internal organization of banks. Mechanisms for communications among banks concerning development of personnel procedures and policies are somewhat limited.

Communications

The American Bankers Association, through its Personnel and Management Development Committee, does provide guidance and opportunity for exchange of ideas at annual meetings. Additionally, the personnel officers in the larger banks in many cities do have more or less formalized groups which meet, usually over lunch, to discuss matters of mutual concern. However, in these and other areas, the communications pattern for reaching the smaller city and country banks is somewhat limited. Large meetings in the banking industry among personnel men usually have as either a direct or ancillary purpose the aid or indoctrination of small banks—and the sharing with them of the experiences of the large organizations. However, the effectiveness of this is limited. In the first place, such meetings are usually ill-attended by the smaller banks which, like smaller organizations everywhere, often cannot afford to send men to participate. In the second place, experience is always one of the most difficult things to communicate, especially when environmental differences exist which require that the communication be understood at some level of abstraction.

Managerial Reactions

Because of the variation in the structure which exists in the banking industry, because of its extent, and because of the lack of a mechanism to provide a concerted response pattern on the part of bankers to questions concerning Negro employment, considerable divergence does exist within the industry. The degree of sophistication exhibited by personnel men varies tremendously, and as a result it is often difficult to separate the normal response pattern of the industry from any number of differently motivated responses. Bankers from different areas of the country or representing banks of different sizes will view and interpret differently not only their environmental conditions, but also the strengths of the stimuli which are impinging upon them concerning Negro employment. We know, for example, that some bankers are overreacting to the thrust of government pressures. Fearing further constraints on their managerial prerogatives, they have grown defensive and will not change employment policy until specifically required to do so. Similarly, we know that some bankers have overreacted to the black militancy visible in the news media, and that others have improperly estimated the organizational and economic costs of hiring Negroes.

This lack of communications patterns and possible overreactions on the part of bank managements have greater effect on the smaller banks than on the more sophisticated, city institutions. This is undoubtedly one of the factors which explains why the greatest divergence in apparent policy responses is based on size of institution rather than on location or on the Negro population of the area in which the bank operates.

CONCLUDING OBSERVATIONS

Aside from the slow start of the banking industry in providing meaningful job opportunities to Negroes, the policy patterns exhibited by the industry reflect consideration and concern for furthering the state of Negro economic advance. If the present hiring rates continue, and if the affirmative patterns exhibited by the industry leaders continue, then there will be few areas for continued concern. Over the next several years, in addition to continuing the progress begun, there seem to be three areas which will be of critical importance.

First, the industry must work toward developing a more effective methodology for bringing the smaller banks into the mainstream of thinking on banking personnel activities in racial relations. Second, the industry must work toward devising methodologies for recruiting or training greater numbers of Negro executive personnel. Third (a point covered in a previous chapter), the industry must determine the extent to which it will be willing to participate in social responsibility outside of the employment sphere. The continuing urban orientation of the industry will require that it give attention specifically to urban problems. There will be a variety of pressures on the industry attempting to influence it to devote its considerable talents to one specific urban problem rather than another. To those, we shall additionally suggest one which is not often mentioned. We suggest that the industry give consideration to establishing closer relationships with local school systems, where that is possible, and try to act toward influencing the quality of the output of the city schools. Finally, in this and other areas of urban involvement, we recommend that the industry act in a concerted fashion so as to be able to derive the additional publicity and recognition benefits possible from those actions.

Appendix A

SURVEY PARTICIPANTS

During the Summer and Fall of 1968, the author visited fifty banks of various sizes, but all of them large, located in seventeen cities throughout the country. Not all of the banks visited provided usable statistical information. One of the fifty was the Federal Reserve Bank in Philadelphia. As Federal Reserve banks are not subject to Executive Order 11246 or other employment regulation by the Treasury Department, data collected on employment there is not included (although it was much appreciated by the author).

In a different vein, two southern commercial banks, one in Atlanta and the second in Dallas, were unwilling, despite careful introductions and the availability of local and national references of some worth, to provide information—statistical, opinion, or otherwise—in person, by phone, or by mail. A fourth bank, located in another southern city, provided opinions but no statistical data. It is for this reason that the number of "surveyed banks" seen from time to time in the study varies. Usually it is forty-six for statistics, and forty-seven for opinions.

In all of the interviews, the degree of friendliness or cooperation extended the author, while always high, was generally speaking, directly proportional to the level of Negro employment in any given bank. The case could therefore be structured that the employment picture presented by the sample banks is overstated to the degree that these three survey members would provide no data. However, external statistical sources indicate that racial employment at all of these particular three was about on a par for their areas, so the effect here is not large, and should not affect the statistics. Left, then, are statistics from forty-six major bank interviews (and opinions from forty-eight).

The banks which did participate in the survey responded to a structured interview comprising a minimum of sixty questions and requiring from one to three hours to complete. Tabulations of the responses to those questions are included in various places in the study, and specific insights provided by the interviewees are quoted from time to time. Special pains have been taken to insure that no bank is identified with any of the positions taken by this study, or is identifiable from them.

The banks which are listed on the following pages are those which were kind enough to participate in the survey. The author is particularly grateful to them for their time, cooperation, and insights. They are listed by assets and rank, as of June 1968.

SURVEY PARTICIPANTS

Banks	1968 Assets ($ Million)	National Rank
1. Bank of America (San Francisco)	22,357	1
2. First National City Bank (New York)	18,153	2
3. Chase Manhattan Bank (New York)	18,087	3
4. Manufacturers Hanover Trust (New York)	9,588	4
5. Chemical Bank (New York)	8,588	6
6. Continental Illinois National Bank and Trust Company of Chicago	6,595	8
7. First National Bank of Chicago	5,751	9
8. Security First National Bank (now Security Pacific: Los Angeles)	5,487	10
9. Wells Fargo Bank (San Francisco)	4,788	11
10. Crocker Citizens National Bank (San Francisco)	4,248	12
11. United California Bank (Los Angeles)	4,225	14
12. Mellon National Bank (Pittsburgh)	3,860	15
13. National Bank of Detroit	3,537	17
14. The Cleveland Trust Company	2,282	19
15. The First Pennsylvania Banking and Trust Company (Philadelphia)	2,213	21
16. Philadelphia National Bank	1,962	22
17. Detroit Bank and Trust Company	1,882	23

SURVEY PARTICIPANTS
(Continued)

Banks	1968 Assets ($ Million)	National Rank
18. Harris Trust and Savings Bank (Chicago)	1,807	24
19. Manufacturers National Bank of Detroit	1,799	25
20. Seattle-First National Bank	1,748	26
21. Republic National Bank of Dallas	1,636	28
22. Pittsburgh National Bank	1,566	31
23. First National Bank in Dallas	1,487	34
24. Union Bank (Los Angeles)	1,464	35
25. Girard Trust Bank (Philadelphia)	1,451	36
26. The Citizens and Southern National Bank (Atlanta)	1,390	38
27. Wachovia Bank and Trust Company (Winston-Salem)	1,388	39
28. National City Bank of Cleveland	1,319	40
29. Valley National Bank (Phoenix)	1,318	41
30. The Fidelity Bank (Philadelphia)	1,238	43
31. Central National Bank of Cleveland	1,108	47
32. Maryland National Bank (Baltimore)	943	57
33. The Riggs National Bank (Washington, D.C.)	877	64
34. The First National Bank of Atlanta	812	72
35. First National Bank of Arizona (Phoenix)	742	76
36. American Security and Trust Company (Washington, D.C.)	701	84
37. First and Merchants National Bank (Richmond)	698	86
38. First National Bank of Maryland (Baltimore)	638	89

SURVEY PARTICIPANTS
(Continued)

Banks	1968 Assets ($ Million)	National Rank
39. National Bank of Washington (D.C.)	540	106
40. First National Bank of Denver	530	109
41. Denver United States National Bank	471	123
42. State-Planters Bank of Commerce and Trusts (Richmond)	425	140
43. People's National Bank of Washington (Seattle)	400	148
44. The Arizona Bank (Phoenix)	324	180
45. The Colorado National Bank of Denver	287	193
46. Mercantile Safe Deposit and Trust Company (Baltimore)	229	233
47. The Central National Bank of Richmond	205	260

Source of assets and rankings: *Bankers Directory: The Bankers Blue Book.* Final 1968 ed. (Chicago: Rand McNally and Company, 1968), pp. 68-69.

Appendix B

NEGRO BANKING

INTRODUCTION

In a slave society, almost as a matter of definition, the subjugated faction has considerable difficulty in acquiring wealth or engaging in entrepreneurial activities in competition with the slave-owning class. But when slavery gives way to segregation, or when under slavery the prohibitions against economic activities are not severe, the suppressed are often allowed or even encouraged to take over the jobs generally considered to be unglamorous. At one time, unglamorous jobs included any sort of production or trading activity, but in recent history they have been more specialized to manual labor, personal service, and supply activities to their fellows of the same caste. Negroes in this country subsequent to emancipation were very definitely at a severe competitive disadvantage to whites in all job categories, but the pressures were somewhat less severe for these unglamorous categories.

Lack of freedom in job opportunity is not without its mitigating aspects if it is based on a mutually exclusive principle. If barbering, tailoring, cooking, or catering, for example, are considered to be the personal service jobs which should be left to Negroes, and they are in fact left to Negroes, then the opportunity for excellence and for a reputation of some sort is possible to a Negro going into one of those trades. The reputation of Jewish domination of money-lending (as differentiated from banking) owes its origins to such practices in medieval Europe, where the handling of money was considered beneath the dignity of the aristocracy.

Unfortunately (or perhaps fortunately in the long run) for American Negroes, the great in-migration of central and western Europeans towards the close of the last century brought men of low aristocratic pretention who, willing to compete for the jobs previously considered inferior, prevented the formation of Negro "monopolies" in any particular trades. In some occupations concerned with supplying goods and services to the Negro communities, however, Negroes still held a competitive advantage. Bank-

175

ing was one such service. Certainly a Negro banker, especially in his role as a provider of funds, is a source of greater potential understanding as well as a symbol of race pride to the Negro community.

The market for Negro banking until after the turn of the century was one subject to parallel development, a modification and outgrowth of the earlier mutually exclusionary principle. The white bankers were afraid of Negro borrowers and uninterested in Negro depositors. The institutional handling of Negro funds was to be left in the hands of Negroes, and Negro banking was to be encouraged. Many now are surprised by the number, but there have been, to date, at least 135 banks owned and operated by Negroes for Negroes in this country since 1888.[110]

Many factors appeared amenable to Negro banking in addition to its being a profession made possible by white disinterest. Banking provided an outlet in the Booker T. Washington sense for the Negro elite, as the prestige of the banker's job was open to any Negro able to organize and capitalize it. The initial capital required for any small bank was not excessive, and we shall see shortly that there were some Negroes who had managed to accumulate reasonably large fortunes. Because banking has no requirements for raw materials, selling on the open market, or using commercial channels of distribution, founding a bank was not subject to the same sorts of restrictions that manufacturing or trading operations were under segregation.

Unfortunately, the experiment in independent Negro banking was not entirely successful. Negro banks suffered severely from infant mortality, and for the seventy-five Negro banks which failed prior to 1936 whose life spans we know, the average life was only 8.9 years. In bankruptcy, many were unable to recover sufficient assets to provide any dividend for depositors at all. Few were able to provide for over 50 percent dividend.

---

[110] According to one source (Robert Kinzer and Edward Sagarin, *The Negro in American Business* (New York: Greenburg Publisher, 1950), p. 102), the *Negro Year Book of 1912* compiled some 103 institutions operating under the title of "banks." We are able to confirm directly only about a quarter of this number. Our data show forty-nine Negro banks had been founded by this date, of which twenty-seven remained in operation. We suspect that the *Negro Year Book of 1912* included all banks which had been founded and, additionally, all savings and loan associations. The numerical progression of Negro savings and loan associations has been largely lost to history, but the first was founded in Portsmouth, Virginia in 1883, and eighty of them were reported by Kinzer and Sagarin as operating in 1929.

In this Appendix we shall examine the history of Negro banking, and analyze the reasons for its lack of success. Some twenty Negro banks do exist today, but half of those have been founded since 1963. Only six can trace their origins to before the Second World War. This indicates something of a resurgence in this area of Negro endeavor, and we shall also evaluate the modern Negro banks.

To understand the circumstances connected with the rise of Negro banking and to evaluate some of the investment decisions made, we shall have to examine some aspects of Negro life going back to before the Civil War.[111]

The Development of Negro Wealth

Before the Civil War, real estate constituted the chief type of wealth in the southern part of the country, and some of this was in the hands of Negroes. Negro property-owning traces its origin back at least as far as one John, of Lancaster, a free Negro who was assessed for eight acres of land and a horse by the Pennsylvania tax levy of 1779.

By 1960, when the ratio of Negroes to the total population of the country was actually higher than it is today, a fair number, though not a large proportion, of Negroes were freedmen or progeny of freedmen,[112] and the extent of their wealth was respectable. Harris points this out in an example from Louisiana:

> At New Orleans in 1836 there were 855 free Negroes who owned 620 slaves and other property assessed at $2,462,470. By 1963 their holdings had increased about fourfold. In appealing to the State in that year for permission to exercise

---

[111] Here and subsequently in this section, I am deeply indebted to Dr. Abram L. Harris, late Professor of Economics at Howard University and the University of Chicago, whose book, *The Negro as Capitalist*, written in 1936, I have drawn from heavily. Dr. Harris's work is beautifully constructed, scholarly, objectively neutral in tone, and well worth the reading if copies can yet be found. (It is apparently being reprinted and should soon be available again.) In the balance of this section, I have footnoted Dr. Harris only for direct quotes, but almost all of my historical material is taken from him, as his is the only detailed source extant on the subject. (Philadelphia: The American Academy of Political and Social Science, 1936.)

[112] The first census of the United States, in 1790, showed 757,208 Negroes who constituted 19.3 percent of the total population. Seven point nine percent of the Negroes were Free Negroes. By 1860, the census of that year showed the percentage of Negroes to the total population had fallen to 14.1 percent and their numbers were 4,441,830. Eleven percent, or 488,070, were Free. These data are found in Kinzer and Sagarin, *op. cit.*, p. 27.

the right of suffrage these "gens de couleur" claimed that they paid taxes on more than nine million dollars' worth of property. This was hardly an overstatement of their wealth because in 1860 the value of the slaves and real estate held by the wealthy free Negroes of Louisiana was variously estimated at from ten to fifteen million dollars.[113]

Apparently, the Negroes in Louisiana were particularly prosperous, but not uniquely so. The estimated five hundred thousand free Negroes in the country at the eve of the Civil War had real and personal wealth at their command conservatively said to amount to $50,000,000, of which half was in the southern states. In addition, Harris estimates that one in five of the free Negroes had obtained manumission through self or family purchase, adding at least $10,000,000 to the total wealth owned which was none the less real for its odd form.[114]

Outside of agrarian operations, the free Negro entrepreneurs were engaged in generally small operations of the personal service sort, such as barbering, running livery stables, tailoring, cooking, saloon keeping, catering, and the like. Merchandising and manufacturing, commercial undertakings requiring skillful bargaining, accounting, and capital, were uncommon, although individual accounts can be found of Negroes operating such diversified trades as coal dealing, sail-making, and agricultural machinery manufacturing.

The financial position of the free blacks before and after the War was ever precarious, although there were some notable exceptions, such as Cyprian Ricaud, a plantation owner in Iberville Parish, Louisiana, whose wealth included ninety-one slaves in 1851, or Thomy Lafon whose estate at his death in the late nineteenth century was assessed at a half-million dollars. The more common state of affairs was widespread poverty, which led to the organizing of a number of mutual assistance societies, often but not always of a fundamentally religious or social nature. The earliest of these, the Free African Society, dates to 1778, and by 1850 it had become the first of over 100 societies with a membership approximating 8,000. The rapid growth of these societies indicates that they were obviously being responsive to a felt need. Operating as mutual funds, they generally provided sick benefits and death payments on the basis of monthly dues of about

---

[113] Harris, *op. cit.*, p. 8.

[114] *Ibid.*, p. 9.

twenty-five cents per member. Some were large enough to maintain deposits in commercial banks, but they generally did not lend or invest funds, leaving this function within the community to a few individual Negro money lenders and note discounters.

Until the Civil War, these last named individuals were about the only source of credit to Negroes. White banks, savings banks, and home building associations frequently denied them the privilege of even becoming depositors. Sometimes this denial was effected by the charter of the institution and sometimes by enactment of the state legislatures. In Harris's words:

> Undoubtedly race prejudice was at the root of these discriminations. Yet when it is remembered that the majority of free Negroes controlled only small sums of money and that the cost of carrying their deposits was relatively great, banks may have had an economic reason for excluding them in many cases.[115]

We shall see subsequently that Harris's observations on the size of deposits and their cost may not have been unfounded.

As borrowers, too, Negro merchants undoubtedly had great difficulty securing credit, although in view of the variety of businesses conducted, at least some source of institutional money had to be available to them. Then as now, the lack of credit facilities for capitalization of specifically Negro enterprises was held to be a cause for serious anxiety, and as early as 1851 a convention of colored people met in New York to discuss forming a bank to provide credit for Negro homesteaders and entrepreneurs. By the outbreak of the Civil War, several other plans to the same end were afoot in New York, Philadelphia, and elsewhere, but none of them came to fruition.

With emancipation, the specific obstacle of slavery gave way to the common obstacles to economic advancement of the poor, which were shared by the majority of Negroes: (1) low wages and high competition for jobs; (2) civic and educational handicaps; and (3) the difficulty of obtaining capital and credit. Many felt that the greatest of these was the last.

A few years after emancipation the stage was set for the birth of Negro banking. Slowly, but surely, some Negroes were managing to accumulate funds, either individually or jointly, for which they desired a depository. An economically-based class

---

[115] *Ibid.*, p. 22.

structure was developing rapidly with a Negro elite arising from the operation of service enterprises, or, less frequently, from real estate ownership and operation. But so far, there had been little Negro experience with banks as such. This was to come with one of the grand experiments of the reconstruction period, the Freedmen's Saving and Trust Company.

THE FREEDMEN'S BANK

The organization of the Freedmen's Bank is very closely tied with the usage during the War of military banks as depositories for the savings of Negro soldiers. Whether because of the required allotment system sometimes used, or from thrift, many of the colored soldiers desired a place to store all or a portion of their wages until the end of the war. To satisfy this need, several generals organized military banks, which also came to be used by Negroes outside the army. At War's end these banks had accumulated upwards of $200,000 of unclaimed deposits of Negro soldiers who had died or disappeared, and feelings arose that a permanent savings bank should be formed to protect these deposits and to serve the general financial interests of the Negro populace. Congress acted, and on March 3, 1865, President Lincoln signed the bill creating the Freedmen's Savings and Trust Company, subsequently renamed the Freedmen's Bank.

The Freedmen's Bank began auspiciously. By March 1866, it had accumulated over $185,000 from the military banks and sufficient general business from its fourteen branches to have a balance due depositors of some $200,000. By 1872, there were at least 70,000 depositors scattered over the Southeast, and the bank held deposits of over $3.6 million. By 1873, deposits had grown to $4.2 million, a level which would not again be reached in Negro banking until the First World War. In 1874, the bank failed. It failed owing $2,939,925.22 to some 61,131 depositors who between 1875 and 1883, were able to recoup only 62 percent of their funds as dividends in bankruptcy.

The Freedmen's Bank was not a typical banking institution. It held a special congressional charter and was outside the National Banking Act of 1864. It was managed by trustees, with no stockholder capital. It was allowed to open and operate branches but was not meant to engage in general banking. Its investment potential was initially circumscribed, and two-thirds of its deposits were to be in government bonds, with the remaining to be left as an "available fund." It was not supervised and no security was required of its officers nor penalty provided for their misconduct. Because of the nature of its founding, it was able to attract many depositors by cloaking itself with an "official" character hinting strongly at government sponsorship.

Neither was the Freedmen's Bank a typical Negro bank. It was run, presumably, *for* Negroes (although it never restricted its business specifically to that race), but in the beginning it was not run *by* Negroes, and until 1870, few Negroes were employed in any capacity. It was meant to be a philanthropic venture into mutual trust savings under the control of public-spirited white citizens who, as officers and trustees, were to look upon their services as contributions to a charitable cause and were therefore to receive no loans, wages, or any other remuneration save necessary expenses.

Both the character and the charter of the bank were changed during the nine years of its existence: the charter not until 1874, but the character beginning in 1866. The panic of 1873 should not have affected the bank as much as many smaller banks, but the "reckless speculation, overcapitalization, stock manipulation, intrigue and bribery, and downright plundering" rampant in the country between 1866 and 1873 were reflected in the activities of the bank's management.[116]

After 1870, the bank was headed by H. D. Cooke, who was also president of the First National Bank of the District, and a cousin of Jay Cooke, the nation's leading private banker. When Jay Cooke's Northern Pacific bond venture fell through in 1873 and his own bank failed, it took with it his cousin's First National Bank of the District and set off the violent phase of the panic of 1873. The tie-in was direct, as the Freedmen's Bank was being used by the First National as a source of funds for both the firm and its officers and a repository of worthless paper. The Freedmen's Bank did not survive H. D. Cooke. When the First National failed, the failure precipitated runs on the Freedmen's Bank, which had come to be looked on as sort of branch of Jay Cooke. In eighteen months, the Bank lost $2 million in deposits, and although it remained open under the new management of the famous Negro leader, Frederick Douglass, the doors were closed by him on June 28, 1874.

---

[116] *Ibid.*, p. 33.

The Freedmen's Bank failed not only because of the speculation and dishonesty of its previous management, but also because of its high operating expenses and heavy investment in fixed, illiquid assets, notably real estate. Considerable assets had been tied up in office buildings and furniture.

The important aspects of the failure of the Freedmen's Bank have been summed up as follows:

> The country began to be filled with rumors, usually based on fact, concerning the state of affairs of the Freedmen's Bank, and there were consequently runs on the bank. The business depression, lower realty value, corruption, stealing, disregard for the interests of the depositors, and manipulation of funds—these were the combining factors in bringing about the end. The controlling banks themselves failed, and the trustees, who had deposits in the bank and knew of its coming failure, were quick to withdraw their money, while they continued to solicit the funds of the Negroes. And *because the bank was identified with the endeavors of the newly-freed Negro, anyone who dared to raise a cry against the mismanagement was charged with being anti-Negro;* inasmuch as the enemies of the Negro were not interested in the bank, and the friends were effectively silenced with the anti-Negro charge, there was no exposure of the condition of the bank.[117]   (Emphasis added.)

Despite its failure and its failings, the operation of the bank subsequent to 1870 had some value as a training ground for a few Negro bookkeepers, clerks, and tellers; and it provided a means of acquainting Negro shopkeepers and other businessmen with "high finance." It also encouraged thrift and the acquisition of property among Negroes, not only in the home offices in New York and Washington but throughout the South, wherever its thirty-three branches were located.

With the failure of the Freedmen's Bank, Negroes were again left without an institutional financial structure. The wealthy Negroes and those with adequate collateral were generally able to participate in the white organizations as depositors or borrowers. But the white banks' continued unwillingness to serve the needs of the small Negro saver left this class again demanding institutions geared to them. Harris presents these views perhaps more cogently:

---

[117] Kinzer and Sagarin, *op. cit.*, pp. 63-64.

White banks, it was more and more alleged, would not supply the Negro businessman with necessary capital and credit. In consequence, Negro leaders maintained that the organization by Negroes of their own banking facilities would meet this need. The degree to which white banks have been motivated in this attitude by racial instead of economic considerations is hard to determine, but from our investigation we do know that the policy of many white banks is to discourage the deposit business of Negroes as a general rule. The adoption of this policy has been attributed by several white officials to two main causes. The first is the probability of losing the large business of white clients who refuse to patronize public establishments frequented by Negroes in large numbers. The second and more important cause is the high cost involved in handling the deposit accounts of Negroes whose monthly balances are as a rule below the average and whose withdrawals are unusually heavy and frequent.[118]

This was answered by the rise of the Negro banks.

NEGRO BANKS

The great surge in banks operated for Negroes by Negroes began in 1888 and ended with the great depression, roughly forty years later. During those forty years, records show at least 135 Negro banks were founded. All save nineteen of these had failed by 1933, and only six of that group remained in 1958.

The progression in the number of Negro banks is shown in Figure B-1, and the progression of aggregate total resources, as far as they are known, in Figure B-2. These figures make apparent that the relative prosperity of Negro banking institutions, at least as measured by total resources and the number of foundings and failures, was not highly dependent on general economic conditions. Except for the period 1910-1915, in fact, the growth or retraction of Negro banks seem countercyclical. Six institutions were founded during the year of the great panic of 1907, for example, and twenty-two Negro banks failed during the five years of prosperity preceding the Great Depression of 1929. Some other factors were obviously involved in the failure of these banks, and actually there is enough commonality among the 129 failures to admit of some tentative generalizations.

[118] Harris, *op. cit.*, p. 54.

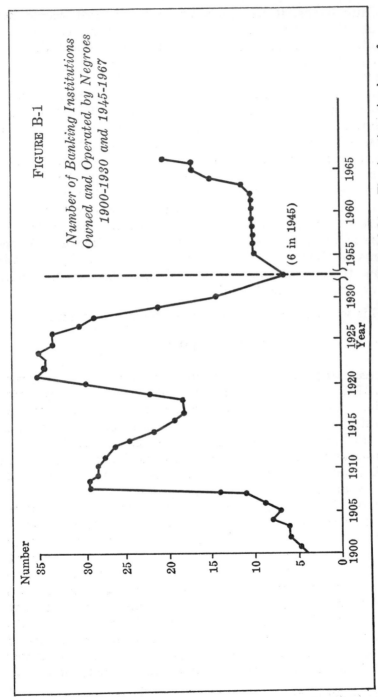

FIGURE B-1

*Number of Banking Institutions
Owned and Operated by Negroes
1900-1930 and 1945-1967*

Source: 1900-1930: Abram L. Harris, *The Negro as Capitalist* (Philadelphia: The American Academy of Political and Social Science, 1936), Appendix IV.

1945-1967: National Bankers Association

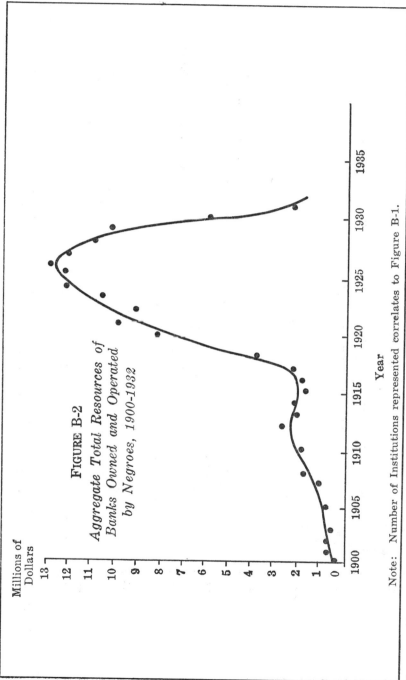

FIGURE B-2

Aggregate Total Resources of Banks Owned and Operated by Negroes, 1900-1932

Note: Number of Institutions represented correlates to Figure B-1.

Source: Abram L. Harris, *The Negro as Capitalist* (Philadelphia: The American Academy of Political and Social Science, 1936), Appendix IV.

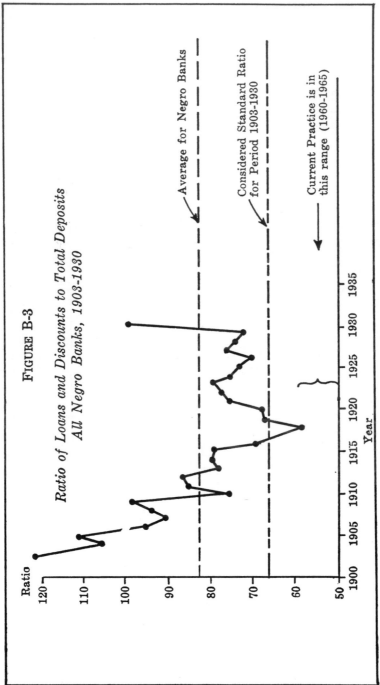

FIGURE B-3

Ratio of Loans and Discounts to Total Deposits
All Negro Banks, 1903-1930

Source:　Abram L. Harris, *The Negro as Capitalist* (Philadelphia:　The American Academy of Political and Social Science, 1936), Table VI.

Negro Bank Failures

Among the factors which most often contributed to the failure of the Negro banks were overexpansion of loans, accepting often worthless securities and real estate as collateral which resulted in an overcommitment to illiquid investments; misconception of the nature of banking, ignorance of banking methods, and pilfering and fraud on the part of bank officers; and an inability to develop a sufficient mercantile and industrial deposit business. We shall look at each of these in turn.

Loans and investments.—Figure B-3 shows the ratio of loans and discounts to total deposits for the Negro banks between 1900 and 1930. Current banking practice (1968-1969) shows this ratio to be on the order of 50 to 60 percent, but in 1928, 66 percent was considered to be a sufficiently conservative norm.[119] The average for the Negro banks was almost invariably above the "normal" figure, and the average for all of them over the twenty-eight years was 82.6 percent loans to deposits. In other words, in comparison to the standard practice of the times, the Negro banks evidenced a tendency to expand loans and discounts disproportionately to total deposits. Partially this was the result of an inability to secure sufficient deposits, a point we shall return to, and partially from a desire to maximize returns.

In conjunction with a tendency to accept real estate and worthless or illiquid bonds from bank-related or subsidiary real estate-based concerns as collateral, this loan policy had the effect of debasing and solidifying the bank's asset structure, and reducing or eliminating its flexibility in fielding the vagaries of the economy.

As we have seen earlier in this section, much of the wealth accumulated by Negroes prior to 1900 was in the form of real estate. There were few Negroes in manufacturing or merchandising above the retail store level, and as a result marketable securities of corporations were not commonly held, even among the affluent. Among the poor, the only "investment" was in mutual death benefit associations or other fraternal or social organizations. Some of these associations formed their own Negro banks to act as depositories of their funds, and at least four of these banks failed when their officers proved unable to disassociate themselves from the associations or treat them in a businesslike way.

---

[119] *How to Analyze a Bank's Statement* (Bankers Publishing Company, 1928).

Real estate speculations had their effect as well. Three Negro banks were helped to failure through investment in bonds of theater-owning real estate corporations which proved unable to operate their properties at a profit. But the real culprit was often simply the inability of Negro borrowers to provide property other than real estate as collateral. Much of the property tendered was overvalued and many cases have been uncovered of property subject to prior lien being accepted as collateral by inattentive loan officers.

More generally, the problem was simply one of too many fixed and unproductive assets. A difficulty ancillary to this was the understandable desire on the part of most Negro bank managements to add to their aura of prestige and respectability by buying luxurious bank buildings and furnishings, which were often out of scale with the volume of business conducted. At times this sort of real estate absorbed 40 percent of the bank's total assets.

Except for the largest of the Negro banks, such as the Douglass National Bank in Chicago, almost none of them held any substantial amount of government bonds or readily marketable securities as investments. An example is provided by the Binga bank, also a large Chicago bank. When this bank failed, it held a total of only about $45,000 worth of negotiable securities as investments plus fifty-nine loans secured by some $85,000 of industrial stocks and bonds. The total of 861 loans outstanding amounted to a little over a million dollars which included $283,-000 in unsecured notes and $671,000 of loans secured by real estate. Additionally, $800,000 of the bank's resources were tied up in mortgages on Negro property. None of this real estate was particularly salable in 1930, and it is no wonder that the bank could not meet its obligations. It would probably have been in serious trouble even without the help of the $379,000 of unsecured loans made through dummy accounts to ventures in which the president was personally interested.

Deposit structure.—We shall take up the questions of dishonesty and incompetence in the next section, but before we do there is one more operational factor of the Negro banks' business which deserves mention, and that is the general structure of deposits in these institutions.

The Negro banks were never large. The average of total deposits per bank did not rise above $100,000 until after the First World War, and the maximum, in 1929, was scarcely above $350,000 per bank. This included demand deposits, savings deposits, and time and demand certificates of deposit. Besides being small in absolute size, the deposits were ill-structured. A few examples should suffice.

The Savings Bank of the Grand Fountain United Order of True Reformers was one of the first Negro banks. It existed from 1888 until 1910. At the time of its failure, there were 5,500 depositors. The average deposit was only $31.80. There were a large number of deposits of $2.00 or less, and only one private account of more than a thousand dollars.

The Mechanics Savings Bank was one of the largest of the Negro banks, and was organized in Richmond in 1902. When it failed in 1922, its deposits aggregated almost half a million dollars. The average savings deposit was $180 and the average commercial deposit was $127. But 62 percent of the savings deposits were under $50, and among its commercial accounts were 110 customers (almost 10 percent of the total number) who were allowed to maintain balances which *aggregated* only $49.63.

The Metropolitan Bank and Trust Company was organized in Norfolk, Virginia, in 1919 on the heels of the postwar boom. When it was suspended in 1931, almost 85 percent of its 3,797 depositors were maintaining balances of under $50.00. There were 462 depositors with claims to less than $1.00.

It is easy to demonstrate that the time, and therefore personnel, required in a bank is proportional to the number of transactions rather than the size of transaction. There is very little difference in bank costs between handling a check or deposit for $150.00 or one for fifteen cents. But it is obvious that the profit potentials of the former are much greater.

Unfortunately, no information is available on the relative staffing levels of these Negro banks and white banks of the same size at that time. Nor do we have information on the deposit structures of the small white banks. But certainly the deposit structures portrayed above (which, incidentally, are typical rather than extreme examples) are not conducive to profitable banking.

Dishonesty and incompetence.—It is never pleasant to write of dishonesty and incompetence, to assess guilt, and to assign blame. It is especially unpleasant to speak of it in small banks wherein the traditional widows and orphans, among others, have reposed their trust. But in fact, dishonesty and incompetence have contributed to the failure of, literally, hundreds of banking institutions in this country, and the Negro banks have had their share of both.

Among Negro bank failures, incompetence seems to have played the larger role, although the dividing line between gross neglect and willful misconduct is more difficult to draw than might be imagined.

Many of the Negro banks should not have been chartered in the first place. But state bank departments appear to have been willing to wink at personal speculations by Negro bank officers and at interlocking subsidiaries in the interests of building as "strong" a Negro banking structure as possible to promote "parallel race development."

This racial policy, which was felt to benefit everyone, was especially emphasized in Virginia, North Carolina, and to a lesser degree in the other southern states. It could not be projected if state banking departments gave the impression of not encouraging the Negroes to develop their own institutions.

Although this practice served to reflect and to reinforce the social convictions of the period, it was hardly designed to insure efficient and trustworthy bank managements. As is so often the case when economic institutions overindulge social whims, the long-term exigencies of economics could not be avoided; instead of promoting a sound parallel Negro banking structure, these policies helped to destroy it by destroying its fiduciary credibility.

There were some dishonest men in Negro banking, and indeed, charges were pressed on three or four. But even in these cases there is insufficient evidence to substantiate even an impression that banks were founded for dishonest purposes. The more common pattern consists of large withdrawals from dummy accounts, large unsecured loans to officers, false entries and erasures, or other loose practices in the confusion surrounding the last few weeks of the failing firms. Generally speaking the real damage had already been done through previous mismanagement or poor supervision of employees.

A good deal of the blame for this must be laid simply to lack of training and experience on the part of the managers. And the blame for that must devolve to the white banks, banking institutions, and regulatory authorities. For where were aspiring Negro bankers to acquire the experience with "good banking practices"? Where could they find skilled tellers, bookkeepers, clerks, or other employees? To whom were they supposed to apprentice themselves? Whose experience could they follow in making sound investments?

Even today there are very few Negroes in managerial positions in the white banks; in 1900 there were none. Only in late 1968 was any mechanism established to provide outside training for Negroes working in Negro banks, and that project is still in the experimental stage; in 1900, there was none. The Freedmen's Bank did provide a training ground for a few managers and employees between 1870 and 1873, but the first Negro bank was not established for fifteen years thereafter. There was also very little in the way of self-help. The National Bankers Association, the Negro equivalent of the American Bankers Association, was not founded until 1927. So if confusion of goals resulted, if there were evidences of loose control and bad banking practices, it should not be much of a surprise.

Summary of historical development.—We have seen above that the experiment in Negro banking was not highly successful. For every eight Negro banks formed between 1888 and 1928, one remained in 1936. The failures arose from a variety of causes, but predominant among them were overexpansion of loans; commitment to unproductive and illiquid investments, especially real estate; an absence of commercial and industrial business or other large accounts; and incompetence, dishonesty, and lack of training among bank managers.

Negro banking suffered severe attrition during the late 1920's and was further hurt by the Great Depression; but it did not disappear. By the beginning of the Second World War there remained seven all-Negro banks. Three more were founded in the postwar boom years, 1946 and 1947; one in 1963; four in 1964; two in 1965; and three more in 1967. These banks obviously exist for a different purpose and under different conditions than did their predecessors.

THE MODERN NEGRO BANKS AND THE RATIONALE OF THEIR EXISTENCE

There has been a resurgence in the number of Negro banks in recent years, and that resurgence will undoubtedly continue apace as long as national emphasis and interest centers on and encourages "black capitalism," "black control of black business," and similar philosophies. But separatism is one of only two understandable reasons for Negro banking to exist in the late 1960's.

Separatism

Separatism versus integration has been an issue since emancipation. Frederick Douglass, during the reconstruction phase following the Civil War, attempted to lead his fellows into the mainstream of America. With the help of a still-"abolitionist" congress he sought political and economic equality for Negroes. The road was not easy. Following severe southern reactions around the close of the last century, it became evident that the strengths of a number of economic and sociological factors had been overly discounted. Southern whites were demanding and enforcing segregation. From among the Negroes, two leaders arose who reflected the new realities, albeit in different ways.

Booker T. Washington favored accommodation with the whites together with internal economic development. "His aim was to curry favor, to advance slowly through education and race improvement, to assure the whites that he neither sought nor desired integration for the Negroes.[120] In Washington's words:

> In all things that are purely social we can be as separate as the fingers, yet one as the hand in all things essential to human progress.[121]

Simultaneously with Washington's plea for accommodation, and partially in reaction to it, was W. E. B. DuBois's call for militancy:

> In the decade previous to the First World War, DuBois denounced the spirit of compromise, and demanded that Negroes stand up and fight for their full rights as human beings and as Americans. He called for the advance of Negroes in business, declared that the separate economy was being forced upon the race, but [sic] laid the foundations for a long range program of integration through militant struggle against all compromise.[122]

The arguments for and against separatism continued apace, but by the early 1960's, it seemed the battle had finally been won. The movement towards enforced integration which had

---

[120] Kinzer and Sagarin, *op cit.*, p. 41.

[121] Washington, speech at Atlanta, Ga., quoted by Kinzer and Sagarin from E. Franklin Frazier, *The Negro in the United States* (New York: The Macmillan Company, 1949), p. 41.

[122] Kinzer and Saragin, *op. cit.*, p. 45.

begun on the state level a few years previously was given the sanction of the federal government under which conditions it was more or less grudingly accepted by the majority of the white population. The country at least should have been free of one of the points of the dilemma of separatism versus integration.

Almost immediately, when the dust of change had settled, and to the surprise of many "establishment whites," new, again militant Negroes emerged as leaders under the banner of black power and black separatism. Roy Innis, director of the Congress of Racial Equality at the time of this writing, believes that "integration is as dead as a doornail." [123] Seeking ideological support by drawing analogies between his philosophical stance and that of the revolutionaries of 1776, he is demanding, under threat of revolt and chaos, federal funds for a separate economy.

> . . . We want the transfer of institutions within the black community to the management and control of the people themselves. Nixon should support the concept of community control of schools, welfare, sanitation, fire, police, hospitals, and all other institutions operating in the so-called "ghettos." [124]

Unfortunately, it is the militance which is most visible to the white community in the requests of the Innises and others on the more extreme "Black Fringe." But by association, the white reaction spreads to reject even the arguments of the simple economic separatists. Over recent years most of us have lost sight of the economic arguments, many of them cogent, for separatism—for the society within a society. Unfortunately, Mr. Innis has lost sight of them as well. For now, just as during the Reconstruction period, although to a lesser degree, there is insufficient Negro professional and managerial talent and insufficient Negro capital to make the scheme work even if the overwhelming practical difficulties such as geographic feasibility could be worked out and a consensus could be gained on the merits of the idea. At some stage in the past such a scheme might have worked, but at the moment the offering of it serves no useful purpose and only promotes further interrace bitterness.

The point of all this is that the argument for economic independence which seems to be accepted by many as both new and

---

[123] Interview, "When Negro Leaders Look Ahead . . ." *U.S. News & World Report*, November 25, 1968, p. 60.

[124] *Ibid.*

exciting is, in fact, neither. It is old and pragmatically infeasible, and although the desire for it as evidenced, for example, in the call for "black banks for black people," is in some ways understandable, it is best left unheeded. If there are to be specifically black banks, they need other justification.

Economics and Sociology

To a very large degree it is difficult to find justification for modern black banks. The usual arguments are economic and sociological, and they deserve some attention.

Any functions which Negro banks can perform can be done at least as well by white (integrated) banking firms. There is no longer a need, as existed in 1895 or 1925, for a specifically Negro place of deposit of Negro funds. The white commercial banks, even in the South, have long ago realized that they would not lose white customers by accepting Negro depositors, and by the use of sliding charges on deposit accounts have protected themselves, as have the modern Negro banks, from the onus of too many unprofitable small accounts.

As a source of funds either for personal finances or business capitalization, Negro banks can claim no particular advantages save those arising from a better rapport with and understanding of potential borrowers. And this has its disadvantages as well as benefits, for the possible Negro borrower whose request for a loan is denied for sound banking reasons will be even more disenchanted with a Negro bank which refuses his request for funds than with a white bank where, at least, he can feel his request was denied through the bigotry he has been taught to expect.

Again, concerning funds for slum development or other worthwhile black community projects, which are almost by definition economically high-risk, the Negro banks are still generally too small to participate on any level above tokenism. To illustrate, financing for "Progress Plaza" and "Progress Aerospace Enterprises," two black-owned, black-operated Philadelphia undertakings of Rev. Leon Sullivan sprang from $100,000 seed capital raised by Sullivan himself through his church members to which was added some $2.5 million of construction loans and long-term financing arranged though a major Philadelphia bank.[125] Again,

---

[125] *Evening Bulletin* (Philadelphia), November 21, 1968, and "In the Black," *Philadelphia Magazine*, June 1968, p. 83.

in October, 1958, ". . . five of Manhattan's largest banks agreed to provide up to $50 million to help minority businessmen. A consortium of 23 Houston banks has pledged $7,000,000 for the same purpose, a nine-bank group in Philadelphia, $6,000,000, a group in Boston $3,000,000." [126] Except for the seed capital, which was private rather than institutional Negro money, the other funds mentioned here, over $68 million, are all from white commercial banks.

This is not to demean or to belittle the Negro banks. Their total aggregate resources in 1967 were less than three times the amount pledged above, and it is no more reasonable for them to be involved than it would be for the (hypothetical) Cattle Exchange Bank of Greencastle, Pennsylvania.

The Negro banks are not economic giants, and they have little in the way of discretionary capital available for high-risk ventures. This is seen in Table B-1, which shows the status of this segment of the industry compared with the industry as a whole. In this decade, Negro banks have grown rapidly in numbers and in assets, but taken together they command less than four one-hundred-thousandths of the resources of the industry. Together, in 1967 they were less than one-tenth the size of the Pittsburgh National Bank, which was ranked twenty-eighth in assets by *Fortune's* survey.[127]

There is an argument occasionally raised which takes the position that the shadow of the black banks is larger than they, that their presence causes the regular commercial banks to act differently than they would alone. A passage from an Atlanta study illustrates this point:

> As in the case of insurance, Negro banking has aimed at satisfying a definite need—to provide a range of credit assistance to Negroes. *An important side effect has been to force a reconsideration of loan policies in white banks* which welcome Negro depositors but are generally not interested in extending loan services.[128] (Emphasis supplied)

---

[126] "The Birth Pangs of Black Capitalism," *Time*, October 18, 1968, p. 99.

[127] "The 50 Largest Commercial Banks," *Fortune*, June 15, 1968, p. 208.

[128] Harding B. Young and James M. Hund, "Negro Entrepreneurship in Southern Economic Development," *Essays in Southern Economic Development*, ed. Melvin L. Greenhut and W. Tate Whitman (Chapel Hill, North Carolina: The University of North Carolina Press, 1964), p. 135.

TABLE B-1.   *Resources, Growth Rates, and Size of Banks Owned and Operated by Negroes Relative to All Commercial Banks*
1940-1967

Year	Number of Negro Banks	Total Assets Negro Banks ($ Million)	Asset Growth Negro Banks (Percent)	Total Assets All Banks ($ Billion)	Asset Growth All Banks (Percent)	Negro Bank Assets as Percent of Total
1940	8	Approx. 5.0	—	Approx. 68.0	—	.0074
1960	10	58.0	—	246.8	—	.0235
1961	10	62.7	8.1	254.2	3.0	.0247
1962	10	71.3	13.7	274.2	7.9	.0260
1963	11	76.9	7.9	298.9	9.0	.0257
1964	15	84.0	9.2	325.5	8.9	.0258
1965	17	93.4	11.2	357.2	9.7	.0261
1966	17	106.9	14.5	387.1	8.4	.0276
1967	17	162.2	51.7	421.1	8.8	.0385

Sources: (1) Federal Deposit Insurance Corporation (as reported by National Bankers Association).

(2) National Bankers Association, *NBA Salary Study*. A report prepared for distribution to NBA member banks (Washington: Xeroxed, 1968).

Were this argument valid, of course, those cities in which the commercial banks were faced with the competition of Negro establishments should be as Meccas for black businessmen. However, the authors of the above quote went on in the same paragraph:

> There has been no real competition from white banks for Negro business loans; a survey of major Atlanta banks revealed but few Negro business loans on their books.[129]

One of the largest of the Negro banks is located in Atlanta and has been there since 1921.

Employment

From a sociological viewpoint, one of the most powerful arguments for the black banks is that they provide service to the community as a training ground and place of employment for Negro tellers, bookkeepers, clerical workers, and managers. For all save the last category, this is both insignificant in any sort of absolute terms and unnecessary, at least since 1964. Negro bank employees do apparently receive somewhat higher wages than employees in white banks of similar size, although about the same as the average for all nonsupervisory employees in commercial banking. Negro bank officers salaries are somewhat less than those of officers in similar-sized white banks.[130] These relationships are shown in Table B-2.

To at least some degree these data reflect the fact that, although small when compared with commercial banks, these banks are large and prestigious institutions in the Negro community. There is also the possibility that the figures reflect marketplace considerations. One woman personnel officer from an all-Negro bank reported: "We have a lot of trouble hiring qualified people. They would rather go and work for the big, downtown banks." [131]

This view finds corroboration in the Atlanta Study mentioned previously:

> The barrier to organization of the [new Negro banking] enterprise has been locating persons with training and experience in banking. Negro banks in other cities can ill

---

[129] *Ibid.*

[130] National Bankers Association, *NBA Salary Study.* A report prepared for distribution to NBA member banks (Washington: Xeroxed, 1968).

[131] Interview by the author, Chicago, October 29, 1968.

TABLE B-2. *Average Annual Wage Comparisons*
Negro and Non-Negro Banks

	1966	1967
Officers		
NBA banks (13 all-Negro banks)	$8,539	$9,899
All FDIC banks of under $25 million deposits	9,330	10,072
All commercial banks	N.A.	N.A.
Employees		
NBA banks (13 all-Negro banks)	$3,713	$4,113
All FDIC banks of under $25 million deposits	3,127	3,752
All commercial banks	4,294	4,495

Sources: (1) National Bankers Association, *NBA Salary Study*. A report
prepared for distribution to NBA member banks (Washington: Xeroxed, 1968).

(2) *Monthly Labor Review*, various issues, 1966 and 1967, Table
C-1.

afford to release some of their trained employees in whom
they have made a heavy investment. The problem is made
all the more acute by the fact that Negroes have not been
in responsible managerial positions in banks other than
those operated by Negroes.[132]

The portion of the difficulty laid to regular commercial banks
is treated at length elsewhere. But there is one final reason for
the continued existence of a parallel all-Negro banking structure.
As promised, it is an argument which is understandable, has
considerable validity, and provides a rationale for these banks:
Negro banks provide a comfortable place of employment for
Negro managers, and they provide an outlet for Negro enter-
preneurial activity.

In one view:

The Negro banking industry has long been a source . . . of
race pride. . . . The banker symbolizes, perhaps more than
anyone else, the successful businessman of the community,
and the race, anxious to demonstrate the extent of its suc-

---

[132] Young and Hund, *op. cit.*, p. 136.

cess in the business world, has looked hopefully upon its banking efforts.[133]

In this regard, the Negro banks are not significantly different from a variety of immigrant or other nationalistically-oriented banks. The opportunity to do what one wishes—even to the founding of a bank—should be available to anyone willing to bear the risk. Naturally, if it is a Negro who feels such an urge, the resultant bank will be a "Negro bank." If the institution is successful in competition with the regular commercial banks of the area, certainly no harm has been done and considerable personal and perhaps some sociological good has resulted.

---

[133] Kinzer and Sagarin, *op. cit.*, p. 102.

Appendix C

LEGISLATIVE AND REGULATORY HISTORY
AFFECTING BANKS

Legislation and regulations of American industry relating to equal employment opportunity for all races take three separate forms. Congressional legislation concerning merit employment can trace its history to the Civil Service Act of 1883.[134] For a long period, the application of this act was essentially reserved to outlawing religious discrimination. Congressional action dealing indirectly with racially equal job opportunity was slow during the depression period. Antidiscriminatory references can be found in the Unemployment Relief Act of 1933, the National Industrial Recovery Act of 1933, and others; but it was not until 1940 when the Ramspeck Act sanctified a 1940 Civil Service rule prohibiting racial discrimination that Congress adopted a philosophy of "equal rights for all." [135]

In order to forestall a threatened Negro marching on Washington in 1941, President Roosevelt opened the second phase of the legislative progression on equal employment by issuing Executive Order 8802 on June 25, 1941.[136] This was the first of the important executive orders and created government-wide machinery which was meant to implement a national policy of nondiscriminatory employment and training through the Fair Employment Practices Committee (FEPC) as an independent agency responsible solely to the President. The executive order also began an era in which continued efforts to secure equality of employment opportunity fell almost exclusively within the province of the Chief Executive.

The FEPC was authorized to receive and investigate complaints, but had no direct enforcement powers. It had to rely on moral suasion and negotiation to effectuate any recommendation it made. The FEPC passed out of existence when its funding was not renewed in 1946. And from 1946 until 1961, most of fair employment activities took place in the individual states.

---

[134] The Pendleton Act (Civil Service Act), 22 Stat. 403 (1883).

[135] Ramspeck Act, 54 Stat. 1211 (1940); Exec. Order 8587, 5 Fed. Reg. 445 (1940).

[136] Executive Order 8802, 6 Fed. Reg. 3109 (1941).

During this period, however, two more commissions were created. One was the Committee on Government Contract Compliance, established by Executive Order 10308 on December 3, 1951,[137] and the second was the President's Committee on Government Employment Policy, established by Executive Order 10590 on January 18, 1955.[138] Both of these commissions were replaced on March 5, 1961, by the President's Committee on Equal Employment Opportunity (PCEEO), which was formed by President Kennedy's Executive Order 10925.[139] The Executive Order 10925 (as amended by a subsequent order, 11114)[140] was important not only because it consolidated the government's activities in this area into the hands of a single agency, but also because it required for the first time "affirmative action." (Banks were not subject to this order.)

All told, up until this time, there had been at least nine executive orders (not all of them are cited here) which had some effect on equal employment opportunity. However, there had been no Congressional action since 1940, with the exception of the Civil Rights Act of 1957 which, dealing almost exclusively with voting rights and education, had little effect on employment. Congress finally moved, in 1964, to pass the Civil Rights Act of that year, Title VII of which prohibits discrimination in employment on the basis of race, creed, sex, and national origin. The Act also established the Community Relations Service (now attached to the Department of Justice) and the Equal Employment Opportunity Commission (EEOC).

With Title VII of the Civil Rights Act of 1964 (which became effective in July 1965), came the beginning of increasing complexity involving enforcement of equal opportunity in employment. The EEOC can act only in the event of complaint, must defer to state human relations or fair employment practice commissions, and can only conciliate the parties unless the matter is of sufficient public importance that, through the Attorney General, the courts find it necessary to issue an injunction where discrimination may be found to be intentional. Four groups are thus involved in the enforcement procedure; the individual complaining about discrimination can bring a civil action; the De-

---

[137] Executive Order 10308, 16 Fed. Reg. 12303 (1951).

[138] Executive Order 10590, 20 Fed. Reg. 409 (1955).

[139] Executive Order 10925, 26 Fed. Reg. 1977 (1961).

[140] Executive Order 11114, 28 Fed. Reg. 6485 (1963).

partment of Justice can intervene in that action (or where the Attorney General feels a pattern of discrimination requires a remedy he may bring a civil proceeding of his own) ; the state fair employment practices commissions are expected to enforce their respective laws; and the federal Equal Employment Opportunity Commission has the function of conciliation and persuasion.[141] Notice that this situation is complicated by the fact that the Commission, under the law, is obliged to defer to state action and local laws where such actions and laws are consistent with the objectives of Title VII. Thirty-six states plus the District of Columbia are considered as having enforceable statutes.[142]

Although many considered that the Congressional action in passing the Civil Rights Act of 1964 should have filled whatever legislative vacuum existed, making further executive orders unnecessary, President Johnson responded to pressures placed on him by various civil rights groups and issued Executive Order 11246 less than a year later, on September 24, 1965.[143] This executive order differs from all but a handful of executive orders on all subjects in the past in that it is not a modification or an explanation of existing legislation, but rather has the weight of new law.[144] It is currently the most important tool in the federal arsenal. It abolished the President's Committee on Equal Employment Opportunity, and transferred those functions to the Secretary of Labor. Simultaneously, the Secretary established within the Labor Department the Office of Federal Contract Compliance (OFCC) but continued in effect as a temporary measure the previous rules, regulations, orders, instructions, and directives issued by the President's Committee.

Contractors covered by the order must permit access to their books, records, and accounts "pertinent to compliance with the order, and all rules and regulations promulgated pursuant thereto," during normal business hours.[145] In other ways, too, the

---

[141] Arthur B. Edgewarth, Jr., "Civil Rights Plus Three Years: Banks and the Anti-Discrimination Law," *The Banker's Magazine*, Vol. CL, No. 3 (Summer 1967), p. 26.

[142] *Ibid.*, p. 27.

[143] Executive Order 11246, 30 Fed. Reg. 12319 (1965).

[144] Opinion of a knowledgeable lawyer interviewed by the author in Washington, September 1968.

[145] National Association of Manufacturers, *Summary Analysis of Revised Regulations of the Office of Federal Contract Compliance.* Report prepared

executive order goes far beyond the Civil Rights Act of 1964. It eliminates some of the specific limitations on the authority of the federal government to regulate employment practices in the area of nondiscrimination. The Civil Rights Act does not require "affirmative action" of the kind required by the executive order, and the authority of state agencies administering state equal employment laws is specifically protected by the earlier congressionally established legislation.[146]

One obvious difference between the Civil Rights Act and the Executive Order is that the latter applies only to contractors with the federal government. There had been some question as to whether the relationship between a bank and its depositor is a contractual one. Consequently, Treasury Department regulations were amended, on August 25, 1966, to provide that all banks designated as depositaries of public monies subsequent to November 30, 1966, in accepting them would thereby agree to an amendment of their contract of deposit with the Treasury Department to incorporate an equal employment opportunity clause.[147] This applied to all banks, regardless of the size of deposits, which had more than fifty employees.

The Office of Federal Contract Compliance delegated the burden for insuring the enforcement of Executive Order 11246 to the federal contracting agency having "predominant interest" in the affairs of a particular industry. In the case of the banking industry, this agency is the Department of the Treasury. This brings in the third stage of regulatory pressure on the banking industry; for the Department of Labor (through the OFCC) and the Department of the Treasury (through its contract compliance section) are perfectly within their rights to issue rules, orders, and regulations amplifying or explaining the executive order 11246. In the banking industry, these have primarily taken the form of regulations concerning testing and testing procedures, although in other industries the contracting agencies' requirements have gone considerably beyond those of the

by the law department of the National Association of Manufacturers for distribution to its members (Washington: The Association, 1968), p. 15.

[146] *Ibid.*

[147] "Equal Employment Guidelines for Depository Banks," *Banking* (Journal of the American Bankers Association), (February 1967), p. 47; the amended Treasury Department regulations are found in 31 Fed. Reg. 11388 (1966); their effect on banks can be found in "Guidelines for Compliance by Depositary Banks," 31 Fed. Reg. 15024 (1966).

executive order.[148] To date, the Department of the Treasury has
been content with preparing and distributing suggested drafts of
policy statements and affirmative action programs to be applied
by banks if they so desired.[149] Treasury has also sponsored a
number of conferences and workshops with groups of banks
throughout the country.

The confusion attendant to the administration of Executive
Order 11246 within the contracting agencies is apparent from the
following passage:

> The Secretary has designated an Assistant Secretary as
> the Treasury Department Compliance Officer, who is respon-
> sible to the Secretary for carrying out the duties and re-
> sponsibilities of the Department under Chapter 60 of this
> Title [41] and the provisions of this subpart. In his office
> the Contract Compliance Officer has established an Office of
> Employment Policy, the Associate Director of which is desig-
> nated as the Principle Deputy Contract Compliance Officer.
> He is assisted by Contract Compliance Specialists. Addi-
> tionally, the bureaus and offices of the Department have
> designated Deputy Contract Compliance Officers to assist
> the Department Contract Compliance Officer in the admin-
> istration of the Executive Order, as amended, with respect
> to contractors for whom the respective bureaus and officer
> have been designated as compliance agency units.[150]

Given the duplication of agencies and the complex administrative set-up within each one, it is difficult even to ascertain the
circumstances under which a compliance review might be performed on an individual bank. Apparently, such a review can

---

[148] (Department of Defense) "Defense Contracts Compliance Program:
Factors which Indicate Compliance (No date on publication data) from the
files of the National Association of Manufacturers. This report lists fifty-
five factors which must be specifically met by contractors to indicate compliance. The Atomic Energy Commission has similar requirements: (Atomic
Energy Commission) "Equal Employment Opportunity (Non-Discrimination
in Government Contractor Employment)" TN 4200-26, Chapter 4208, July
21, 1967 (in the files of the commission).

[149] These undated, suggested drafts were issued October 30, 1968, and are
available from the Equal Employment Opportunity Office, United States
Treasury Department, Washington, D. C., 20220.

[150] Text of Treasury Department Regulations, (41 CFR Ch. 60, Sec. 10-
12.802 Administrative Responsibility) found in "Equal Opportunity in Financial Institutions," *Labor Relations Reporter*, Vol. LXX (Jan. 13, 1969),
p. 24.

be initiated by either Treasury or by OFCC. According to an officer with OFCC, in the majority of cases, Treasury will do the initiating, but OFCC can request Treasury to perform a compliance review on a certain bank or group of banks within a certain time period. In either event, the review is actually conducted by Treasury. Subsequent to Treasury's investigation, a report is sent of the results and findings to OFCC for what a Treasury official calls "filing" and what an OFCC official calls "review." [151] In any event, it is possible that OFCC, on reviewing (or filing) the report from Treasury, might be dissatisfied with the conclusions reached. If this is the case, OFCC indicates no unwillingness to reopen an investigation. It is thus possible for an individual institution to be reviewed by both agencies seriatim.

Overall, it is conceivable that an individual bank's activities might be reviewed in succession by a city commission of human relations, a state fair employment practices commission, the Equal Employment Opportunity Commission, the Department of Justice, the Department of the Treasury, and the Department of Labor. Civil suit can also be brought by an individual who feels he might have been wronged. Obviously, the legal and regulatory hierarchy has become extremely complex.

---

[151] Interviews by the author at the Office of Federal Contract Compliance at the U.S. Department of the Treasury, September 20, 1968.

Index

INDUSTRIAL RESEARCH UNIT, DEPARTMENT OF INDUSTRY
WHARTON SCHOOL OF FINANCE AND COMMERCE
UNIVERSITY OF PENNSYLVANIA

Founded in 1921 as a separate Wharton Department, the Industrial Research Unit has a long record of publication and research in the labor market, productivity, union relations, and business report fields. Major Industrial Research Unit Studies are published as research projects are completed. Advance research reports are issued as appropriate in a general or special series.

Major Industrial Research Unit Studies

(Available from the University of Pennsylvania Press or the
Industrial Research Unit)

Gladys L. Palmer, et al., *The Reluctant Job
Changer.* 1962   No. 40 $7.50

George M. Parks, *The Economics of Carpeting and
Resilient Flooring: An Evaluation and Compari-
son.* 1966.   No. 41 $5.00 (Cloth)
                                                           1.50 (Paper)

Michael H. Moskow, *Teachers and Unions: The
Applicability of Collective Bargaining to Public
Education.* 1966.   No. 42 $8.50

F. Marion Fletcher, *Market Restraints in the Retail
Drug Industry.* 1967.   No. 43 $10.00

Herbert R. Northrup and Gordon R. Storholm, *Re-
strictive Labor Practices in the Supermarket Industry.* 1967.   No. 44 $7.50

William N. Chernish, *Coalition Bargaining.* 1969.   No. 45 $7.95

1970 Publications (advance orders accepted)

Herbert R. Northrup, et al., *Negro Employment in
Basic Industry. A Study of Racial Policies in
Six Industries.* (Studies of Negro Employment,
Vol. I)   April 1970   No. 46 $10.00

Armand J. Thieblot, Jr., and Linda P. Fletcher,
*Negro Employment in Finance. A Study of Racial
Policies in Banking and Insurance.* (Studies of
Negro Employment, Vol. II)   June 1970   No. 47 $9.50

Bernard E. Anderson, *Negro Employment in Public
Utility Industries. A Study of Racial Policies in
the Electric, Gas, and Telephone Industries.*
(Studies of Negro Employment, Vol. III)
July 1970   No. 48 $8.50

Nos. I—39 available from Kraus Reprint Co., 16 East 46th St., New York, N.Y. 10017.

Racial Policies in American Industry Report Series

1. *The Negro in the Automobile Industry,*
   by Herbert R. Northrup.   1968 $2.50
2. *The Negro in the Aerospace Industry,*
   by Herbert R. Northrup.   1968 $2.50
3. *The Negro in the Steel Industry,*   1968 $3.50
   by Richard L. Rowan.   (Out of stock)
4. *The Negro in the Hotel Industry,* by Edward C.
   Koziara and Karen S. Koziara.   1968 $2.50
5. *The Negro in the Petroleum Industry,* by Carl B.
   King and Howard W. Risher, Jr.   1969 $3.50
6. *The Negro in the Rubber Tire Industry,* by Herbert R. Northrup and Alan B. Batchelder.   1969 $3.50
7. *The Negro in the Chemical Industry,*
   by William Howard Quay, Jr.   1969 $3.50
8. *The Negro in the Paper Industry,*
   by Herbert R. Northrup.   1969 $8.50 (Cloth)
9. *The Negro in the Banking Industry,*
   by Armand J. Thieblot, Jr.   March 1970 $5.95
10. *The Negro in the Public Utility Industries,*
    by Bernard E. Anderson.   1970 $5.95
11. *The Negro in the Insurance Industry,*
    by Linda P. Fletcher.   1970 $5.95
12. *The Negro in the Meat Industry,*
    by Walter A. Fogel.   1970 $4.50
13. *The Negro in the Tobacco Industry,*
    by Herbert R. Northrup.   1970 $4.50

Other Racial Policies reports will include retail stores, textiles, bituminous coal, trucking, shipbuilding, and railroads among other industries.

Labor Relations and Public Policy Series

1. *Compulsory Arbitration and the NLRB,*
   by Paul A. Abodeely.   1968 $2.50
2. *Union Authorization Cards and the NLRB,* by Alan R.
   McFarland and Wayne S. Bishop.   1969 $2.50

Forthcoming studies will deal with various aspects of government labor policy including bargaining unit determination, picketing and boycott regulation, and government intervention in labor disputes.

Miscellaneous Series

14. *Economics of Carpeting and Resilient Flooring: A Survey of Published Material and a Questionnaire Summary,*
    by David C. Stewart.   1966 $1.00
15. *Job Mobility and Occupational Change: Philadelphia Male Workers, 1940-1960,* by Carol P. Brainerd.   1966 $2.00
16. *Improving the Potential for Negro Employment and Skill Development in the Delaware Valley Fabricated Metals Indutry,* by Armand J. Thiebolt, Jr. and William
    N. Chernish.   1967 $2.00

Order from University of Pennsylvania Press
Philadelphia, Pennsylvania 19104